NO LONGER PROF
SEATTLE PUBLIC

D0355534

PARADOXES OF LIBERAL DEMOCRACY

PARADOXES OF LIBERAL DEMOCRACY

Islam, Western Europe, and the Danish Cartoon Crisis

PAUL M. SNIDERMAN

MICHAEL BANG PETERSEN

RUNE SLOTHUUS

RUNE STUBAGER

PRINCETON UNIVERSITY PRESS
PRINCETON AND OXFORD

Copyright © 2014 by Princeton University Press
Published by Princeton University Press, 41 William Street, Princeton,
New Jersey 08540
In the United Kingdom: Princeton University Press, 6 Oxford Street,
Woodstock, Oxfordshire OX20 1TW

press.princeton.edu

Jacket Illustration: Female Muslim protesters hold a burning Danish flag
during a demonstration in Lahore, Pakistan, February 24, 2006. © Arif Ali/
AFP/Getty Images.

All Rights Reserved

Library of Congress Cataloging-in-Publication Data

Sniderman, Paul M.
   Paradoxes of liberal democracy : Islam, Western Europe, and the Danish
cartoon crisis / Paul M. Sniderman, Michael Bang Petersen, Rune Slothuus,
Rune Stubager.
        pages cm
   Includes bibliographical references and index.
   ISBN 978-0-691-16110-5 (hardcover : alk. paper) 1. Democracy—Social
aspects—Denmark. 2. Freedom of speech—Denmark. 3. Muhammad,
Prophet, –632—Caricatures and cartoons. 4. Caricatures and cartoons—
Political aspects—Denmark. 5. Morgenavisen jyllands-posten. 6. Denmark—
Emigration and immigration—Political aspects. 7. Denmark—Emigration and
immigration—Religious aspects. 8. Islam and state—Denmark. 9. Religious
pluralism—Political aspects—Denmark. I. Petersen, Michael Bang.
II. Slothuus, Rune. III. Stubager, Rune. IV. Title.
   JN7161.S65 2014
   306.209489—dc23   2013035897

British Library Cataloging-in-Publication Data is available

This book has been composed in Charis SIL

Printed on acid-free paper. ∞

Printed in the United States of America

10 9 8 7 6 5 4 3 2 1

TO LISE

Contents

List of Illustrations   ix

Preface   xiii

CHAPTER 1 Introduction   1

CHAPTER 2 A Clash of Rights   10

CHAPTER 3 The Covenant Paradox   52

CHAPTER 4 Flash Point: The Ideological Bases   82
   of Anti-immigration Politics

CHAPTER 5 The Concept of Inclusive Tolerance   117

CHAPTER 6 The Democratic Impulse   141

Appendix A Timeline of the Cartoon Crisis   155

Appendix B Description of the Main Data Set   157

Appendix C Comparison of Respondents from   159
   the Height and Aftermath of the Crisis

Appendix D Scaling and Measurement of   163
   Core Variables

References   167

Index   177

Illustrations

FIGURES

Figure 2.1 Perceptions of Target Groups' Democratic   27
    Commitment and Use of Violence (Scale Scores)
Figure 2.2 Immigrant Attitudes in Denmark over Time,   32
    1993–2007 (Percent Tolerant Responses)
Figure 2.3 Press Coverage of the Issue of Free Speech,   35
    August 2005–August 2006 (Number of Articles)
Figure 2.4 Party Leader Reactions to and Framing of the   40
    Cartoon Crisis, January–June 2006 (Number of Statements)
Figure 2.5 Party Leaders' Framing of the Cartoon Crisis,   41
    January–June 2005 (Percent of Statements)
Figure 3.1 Welfare Attitudes over Time   62
Figure 4.1 Illustration of the Two-dimensional Structure   90
    of the Danish Party System
Figure 4.2 Effects of Positions on the Libertarian-   100
    Authoritarian and Economic Redistribution Dimensions
    for "Perceived Cultural Threat" (Predicted Scores)
Figure 4.3 Effects of Positions on the Libertarian-   102
    Authoritarian and Economic Redistribution Dimensions
    for "Dislike for Muslims" (Predicted Scores)
Figure 4.4 Effects of Positions on the Libertarian-   103
    Authoritarian and Economic Redistribution Dimensions
    for "Perceived Threat from Muslims" (Predicted Scores)
Figure 4.5 Effects of Positions on the Libertarian-   110
    Authoritarian and Economic Redistribution Dimensions
    on the Belief That One "Cannot Be Too Careful in Dealing
    with Other People" (Predicted Scores)

Figure 4.6 Effects of Positions on the Libertarian-   111
Authoritarian and Economic Redistribution Dimensions
on the Belief That "Other People Will Take Advantage of
You" (Predicted Scores)

Figure 4.7 Effects of Positions on the Libertarian-   113
Authoritarian and Economic Redistribution Dimensions
on "Political Knowledge" (Predicted Scores)

Figure 4.8 Percentage of Voters Who Belong to the   115
Traditionalist Left among Mainstream Parties

TABLES

Table 2.1 Immigrant Attitudes in Denmark, Germany,   14
France, the United Kingdom, the Netherlands, and Sweden
(Percent Intolerant Responses)

Table 2.2 Support for Civil Rights of Muslims and Islamic   21
Fundamentalists (Percent)

Table 2.3 Support for the Rights of Target Groups (Percent)   29

Table 2.4 Political Tolerance by Time of Interview, Average   43
for All Groups (Percent)

Table 2.5 Change in Support for Free Speech of Groups from   45
the Height of the Crisis to Its Disappearance from the
Public Agenda (Percent)

Table 2.6 Change in Perception of Threat from Groups from   49
the Height of the Crisis to Its Disappearance from the
Public Agenda (Scale Scores)

Table 2.7 Change in Opposition to Telephone Tapping of   50
Groups from the Height of the Crisis to Its Disappearance
from the Public Agenda (Percent)

Table 3.1 Importance of Welfare Services on Political   58
Consensus Policies by Party

Table 3.2 Importance of Welfare Services on Political   60
Conflict Policies by Party

Table 3.3 Young Mother Experiment: Support for Providing   65
Extra Help with Child Care by Party

Table 3.4 Tougher Requirements Experiment with Young
    Man: Support for Tougher Requirements for Receiving
    Welfare Payments by Party   69

Table 3.5 Tougher Requirements Experiment with Woman
    in Her Fifties: Support for Tougher Requirements for
    Receiving Welfare Payments by Party   72

Table 3.6 Many Children Experiment: Support for Cutting
    Welfare Benefits by Party   74

Table 3.7 Ceiling Experiment: Hurt Immigrants by Party   78

Table 3.8 Ceiling Experiment: Appeal to the Covenant
    by Party   80

Table 4.1 A Test of the Combustibility Hypothesis (Excluding   95
    Danish People's Party Adherents): Effects of Libertarian-
    Authoritarian and Economic Redistribution Positions on
    Anti-immigrant Sentiments

Table 4.2 Replication Tests of the Combustibility Hypothesis: 98
    Danish National Election Studies, 1998–2007

Table 5.1 Group Sympathy by Attitudes toward Immigrants   125
    (Scale Scores)

Table 5.2 Inclusive Tolerance and Civil Rights (Percent in   128
    Highest Third of Supporters of Civil Rights)

Table 5.3 Tougher Requirements Experiment: Support for   133
    Tougher Requirements for Receiving Welfare Payments
    by Attitudes toward Immigrants

Table 5.4 Many Children Experiment: Support for Cutting   135
    Welfare Benefits by Attitudes toward Immigrants

Table 5.5 A Test of the Partisan Ideology Hypothesis   138

Table 5.6 A Test of the Generalized Trust Hypothesis   139

Table A.1 The Distribution of Gender in March–April and   160
    May–July (Percent)

Table A.2 The Distribution of Age in March–April and   160
    May–July (Percent)

Table A.3 The Distribution of County of Residence in   161
    March–April and May–July (Percent)

Table A.4 The Distribution of Education in March–April and   161
    May–July (Percent)

Table A.5 The Distribution of Political Interest in   161
    March–April and May–July (Percent)
Table A.6 The Distribution of Political Knowledge in   162
    March April and May–July (Percent)

Preface

This book is the result of a serendipitous collaboration, reports an un-anticipated discovery, and closes with—to put it at a minimum—a not self-evidently obvious credible conclusion. Together, we will make our case for the unanticipated discovery and not self-evidentally obvi-ous credible conclusion. But here we present an account of the first outcome—the serendipitous collaboration.

Michael, Rune, and Rune—together with their dissertation adviser, Professor Lise Togeby—conceived of this project in June 2005, a little more than two months before the crisis over the place of Islam in Den-mark erupted. The project was kick-started before receiving funding, and fall 2005 was spent on pilot testing questions and survey experi-ments. The gamble paid off. In December 2005, the Danish Social Sci-ence Research Council awarded us a grant. Thanks to months of self-funded preparation, the project got into the field in the first week of February 2006, just as the crisis was going into high gear.[1]

Paul joined the project in 2008, and this book is the product of face-to-face meetings between the four of us, each with a computer in front of him, throwing out ideas, developing measures, drawing out the implications of results, writing postmeeting memos, and then starting the process all over again.

The result has been an account of citizens' capacity for democratic citizenship more optimistic than previous judgments—but not be-cause we believe that previous research is wrong. On the contrary, at every point that comparison between our study and earlier ones is possible, our results are in line with earlier results. Why, then, the

[1] For initial reports on the results of the project, see Petersen et al. 2007a, 2007b, 2007c, 2011a, 2011b; Petersen, Slothuus, and Togeby 2010.

difference between our overall view and that of previous studies of political tolerance?

It is our claim that in long-established liberal democracies, to a degree that has not been recognized, judgments about core political rights are now anchored in consensual rules identifying which controversial groups should be categorized as dangerous or not, and which individuals should be entitled to the benefits of the welfare state or not. Just so far as these rules are consensually agreed on, they are, so to speak, part of the furniture of the political culture. No special acumen or psychological orientation is necessary to put them into effect. These rules, though not always followed with perfect uniformity, tend to be followed by the largest number of people. The outcome is that notwithstanding how most citizens feel about Muslim immigrants, decisive majorities of them support both their civil and social rights.

Ours is not a story of democratic triumphalism, however. Our results, matching those of previous studies, document deep pools of aversion to immigration. They also, again matching those of previous studies, document the strong association between right-wing social values and both aversion to immigration and restrictive immigrant policies. But our focus—and this is the new part that we are proposing—is that some of the values and habits of mind that underpin the unexpected strength of support for the civil and social rights of immigrants are double-edged ones. Paradoxically, they promote equal treatment for some Muslims even as they open the door to discrimination against others.

We have many to thank for this book. The Danish Social Science Research Council (grant number 275–0500195) funded the data collection on which the book is based. At a time when randomized experiments were not part of the standard tool kit of Danish social scientists, the council took a chance and funded this project. The National Science Foundation provided supplemental funding (grant number 0842677 for our Liberal Democracy under Pressure project) to support our five-thousand-miles-apart collaboration.

Many colleagues have provided help and advice during the writing of the book, among them Lene Aarøe, Erik Albæk, James Alt, Jørgen Goul Andersen, Claes de Vreese, Jamie Druckman, Jørgen Elklit, James Gibson, Christoffer Green-Pedersen, Kasper Møller Hansen, Cindy Kam, Hanspeter Kriesi, Lasse Lindekilde, Per Mouritsen, Asbjørn Sonne

Nørgaard, Kim Mannemar Sønderskov, and Jens Peter Frølund Thomsen. Special thanks go to Gitte Sommer Harrits for granting us access to her interviews, which we make critical use of in chapter 4. Along the way, we received skillful research assistance from Merete Arentoft, Bjørn Bjorholm, Jon Hadsund, Morten Pettersson, and Mads Hovgaard Steffensen, and secretarial assistance from Anne-Grethe Gammelgaard, Anna Finderup, and Kate Thulin. Jackie Sargent and Eliana Vasquez should not be held responsible for what Paul has written, but they cannot escape accountability so easily. They should be held responsible for his having written it, since without their encouragement and aid, he would not have managed to do so.

Samuel Johnson memorably quipped, "Depend upon it, sir, when a man knows he is about to be hanged in a fortnight, it concentrates his mind wonderfully." Having the opportunity to present one's results to colleagues in other departments, though admittedly less threatening, has the same beneficial consequences. For opportunities to concentrate our minds, we thank Nuffield College, the international Ethnicity, Immigration, and the French Educational System workshop jointly funded by Oxford University and the French National Center for Scientific Research, the comparative politics workshop in the Department of Politics at Princeton University, the Department of Political Science at the University of Massachusetts at Amherst, and the Department of Political Science at the University of Kansas.

Finishing a book only looks preordained after the book is finished. For helping us cross the finish line, we would especially like to thank Jens Blom-Hansen and Thomas Pallesen. In their role as political science department chairs at Aarhus University, they were able to generously offer funding and other support that enabled us to meet and work together. Another colleague also needs to be singled out. Nelson Polsby once remarked, "Writing is like pulling a rabbit out of the hat but however many times you've done it before, you never know if the rabbit will be there the next time." Just so. And how can one pull off the trick one time after another? There is surely more than one way, but for us, it has been working with our editor, Chuck Myers. Anyone who has the exceptional fortune to work with Chuck knows exactly what we mean.

This book project unfolded while the three younger authors (Michael, Rune, and Rune) were in the midst of establishing families and careers.

We would like to thank our significant others, Helle, Trine, and Kristine, respectively, for their support and encouragement when we left for yet another meeting to nail the paradoxes of liberal democracy. As for the fourth author (Paul), Suz is inseparable from my life.

As a final point, four names appear on the title page, yet we should have included five. The missing name is Lise Togeby, professor of political science at Aarhus University. Lise was the senior researcher of the Aarhus team that conceived, designed, and collected the data on which this book is based. She died before the four of us had our first meeting. It would be wrong, therefore, to make her responsible for what we have done. The best that we can do—little as it is—is to dedicate our book to her.

Lise, the first female professor of political science in Denmark, devoted much of her career to studying the dynamics of tolerance. With this book, we hope to honor her legacy and importance to Danish political science—and to the three of us, her students. She was not just a student of tolerance but rather a practitioner. We owe much to Lise for her continuous support for exploring new and unknown paths as well as her constant encouragement to work hard so as to take part in the conversation of political science at the international level.

PARADOXES OF LIBERAL DEMOCRACY

Chapter 1

Introduction

September 30, 2005, the *Jyllands-Posten*, a newspaper based in Aarhus, a university town in Denmark, published twelve cartoons, some satirizing the prophet Mohammed. The announced reason: the free expression of ideas was being stifled for fear of offending Muslim sensibilities. Now forgotten, or more likely never noticed, many of the cartoons aimed their barbs at those who were complaining of being stifled—mocking the newspaper itself, for example, by showing a boy pointing to a blackboard behind him with an inscription in Persian that "*Jyllands-Posten*'s journalists are a bunch of reactionary provocateurs." Another cartoon caricatured the Danish author who won attention for a book he had under way by complaining of self-censorship, showing him with an orange on his head labeled "PR-Stunt." (Regrettably, the reference to an orange requires a Danish funny bone to appreciate).[1] Still, one cartoon depicted Mohammed with a bomb in his turban, and another showed him shouting to suicide terrorists lining up to enter heaven, "STOP, STOP, we have run out of virgins!" A political firestorm erupted.

This is a study of that political controversy. The reactions of some Middle Eastern governments and religious leaders outside Denmark, not to mention those of some Danish politicians, could not have been better calculated to provoke a backlash against Muslims in Denmark. But there was no backlash. That fact is, by orders of magnitude, our most important finding.

---

[1] The use of the orange in the turban means to get something unexpected and without real effort (i.e., the metaphor is that you walk underneath an orange tree and an orange drops down to you).

It is not immediately obvious why a study of something that did not happen is significant, and still less something that did not happen in a faraway country—a country to admire in many ways, to be sure, but all the same one of background importance strategically and economically. By way of self-promotion, we could respond that what continues to happen—let alone what already has happened—should compel attention. The newspaper that published the cartoons continues to be a target of terrorists. There has been a conspiracy to shoot up its editorial offices, and another to send a letter bomb to blow them up, not to mention repeated efforts to assassinate the cartoonist who depicted Mohammed with a bomb in his turban, with the most recent effort featuring an ax-wielding attacker breaking into the cartoonist's house and attempting to kill him. We could also respond that the issue of self-censorship raised by the publication of the cartoons has crossed over many borders, including those of the United States, most controversially inducing a leading US university press to excise reproductions of the cartoons from a book about the crisis for fear of the violent reaction it might provoke. But these are reasons why a study of the Cartoon Crisis might be engrossing, not why it would be important.

What, then, was our reason for studying it? In our view, a democratic politics cannot escape challenges to civil liberties and civil rights. And the best and perhaps only way to test the sincerity as well as strength of citizens' commitment to the values of a democratic politics is to assess their willingness to defend them in the face of the full headwind of a genuine crisis.

THE STUDY

Libraries are overflowing with multicountry studies of the attitudes of national majorities toward Muslim immigrants. Ours is an exploration of only one country, and what is more, of only one issue that occupied its politics for only a brief period of time: no more than four months and a bit. So it is more than fair to ask, What can this study offer that its many predecessors have not?

Here are four answers as a starting point. The first has to do with the issue itself. The drive to publish cartoons satirizing Islam and the furious reaction to them dramatically symbolized the divide between "us" and "them" in their opposing conceptions of ways of life. From a Danish perspective, what was at stake was a foundational value of liberal democracy: freedom of speech. Foreign governments demanded that freedom of speech had to be subordinated in deference to their values. As if that were not enough, these foreign governments and mullahs also insisted that Danish newspapers apologize, the Danish government acknowledge that Islam had been wronged, and the government take "all necessary measures" to prevent similar affronts in the future.[2]

To say that the furious storm of demands for apologies and self-censorship might provoke defenders of liberal values is akin to asserting that ice storms just might bring down power lines. To reject efforts to impose prior restraints on what a newspaper may publish—as opposed to holding them responsible for what they publish (libel, for example)—is the minimal position that a committed free speech advocate must take. True enough; also reasonable enough as a political position. But there is a perversity to democratic politics. Defending toleration of the expression of ideas with the ardor it deserves, in circumstances like these, can spark intolerance of minorities. Criticizing Muslims for threatening free speech opens the door for those who fear or resent Muslim immigrants out of ignorance or self-interest to join in the hue and cry. Foreign governments insisting on the priority of "their" values on behalf of a foreign religion—how much better can it get for the mobilization of prejudice and chauvinism? The irony is too obvious to miss. Because the crisis was framed as a defense of democratic values, those intolerant of Muslims lucked into a tailor-made opportunity to pass themselves off as defenders of tolerance. And for just this reason, we lucked into a tailor-made opportunity to gauge the full force of their rhetoric when circumstances legitimized anti-Islamic reactions.

The narrative line of the Cartoon Crisis is the clash between the values of liberal democracy—above all, freedom of expression—and the demands of faith—above all, the responsibility of the faithful to protect the honor of the prophet Mohammed. Some extremists aside, this narrative of a "clash of civilizations" is by no means clearly right. At least, it is not apparent to us. Recall the reactions of many in the

[2] Klausen 2009, 70.

United States—including major political leaders—to the exhibition of Andres Serrano's *Piss Christ*, a photograph of a crucifix submerged in urine. And lest there be any suggestion that this is somehow a peculiarly US susceptibility to moralistic outrage, it is worth also recalling that on Palm Sunday 2011, climaxing an "antiblasphemy" campaign, French fundamentalists took hammers and destroyed the photograph when it was on exhibit in Avignon. Yet rightly or wrongly, participants on both sides framed the conflict over publication of the cartoons as a clash between Western and Islamic values. The Cartoon Crisis thus provides an extraordinary opportunity to plumb the challenge of the inclusion of Muslims in western Europe, and above all, assess the reactions of the majority to a Muslim minority in the crucible of a crisis over "special" rights claimed by Muslims.

Another reason for a study of the Cartoon Crisis is the intensity of the conflict. *Crisis* is a term that has suffered abuse from excessive use. The Cartoon Crisis was not a crisis in the sense that the Cuban Missile Crisis was one. There was no mortal peril for entire societies. It was not even a top-of-the-chart political crisis. The governing parties were never at risk of being toppled. Still, diplomatic interventions by foreign governments, an embassy being burned, the staging of demonstrations and boycotts, and the posting of a one million dollar bounty for killing one of the cartoonists all give a legitimacy to the term *crisis*, as do the actions and reactions of Danish politicians. For one, the prime minister pronounced the controversy as Denmark's "worst international crisis since the Second World War." Others railed against foreign interference and Muslims generally. At the least, the Cartoon Crisis provides an opportunity to observe how ordinary citizens react in an extraordinary situation.

Timing is yet another consideration. Studies of citizens' commitment to civil liberties and civil rights characteristically have been carried out *after* the immediate crisis has passed—indeed, usually after a considerable time has passed—and understandably so.[3] It is in the nature of things that one cannot predict when a crisis will erupt, or still less anticipate the particular form it will take. The Cartoon Crisis

---

[3] Samuel Stouffer's (1955) classic study, which was carried out when McCarthyism was at its zenith, is a monumental exception. For important post-crisis-peak studies, see Davis 2007; Brooks and Manza 2013.

serendipitously (for us) had an unusual life history, however.[4] The cartoons were published at the beginning of September 2005. Some diplomatic activities by Middle Eastern governments took place through October, and there were some isolated actions in November and December. But the crisis only boiled over in late January, with the boycott of Danish goods in the Middle East and recall of ambassadors. By then, our surveys were under way. The data on which this study is based thus offer a rare opportunity to observe how ordinary citizens discharge the duties of democratic citizenship at the very time they are under the most stress.[5]

The framing of the issue as a clash between the claims of Islam versus freedom of speech, the intensity of the clash between the two, and the intersection of the timing of the crisis and our study, allowing us to gauge the reactions of the majority to Muslim immigrants at the peak of the crisis, are three advantages that our analysis has enjoyed. And there is one more: how members of a national majority feel about a minority matters; how they treat them matters far more. To what degree do they discriminate against them by opposing the benefits of the welfare society that they will extend to fellow Danes? To what extent do they impose requirements for receiving benefits on Muslim immigrants that they do not impose on fellow Danes? To what extent do they deny them the core rights of democratic citizenship that they willingly extend to fellow Danes? These questions manifestly deserve answers. Now, thanks to the power of randomized experiments, our results can supply responses to these questions—rough-and-ready answers, to be sure, but ones that possess a degree of trustworthiness that traditional studies of public opinion cannot provide.

THE STORY

Our concern is the temper of contemporary liberal democracy. Democracies do face external threats, including some from Muslims. But the internal threats they face go deeper. The test of a democratic politics—the ultimate test, some would argue—is how conscientiously

---

[4] For a detailed account of the development of the crisis, see Klausen 2009. For a detailed timeline, see chapter 2 and appendix A.

[5] For a description of our data, see appendix B.

the majority safeguards the rights of an unpopular minority. The inclusion of Muslim immigrants is currently challenging western Europe. Accordingly, the question at the heart of this study is, How conscientiously will the majority safeguard the rights of Muslims, not in a time of political calm, but rather in light of a storm of demands by Muslims that the claims of their faith trump the values of liberal democracy?

There is no shortage of evidence to back skeptics of the democratic idea. The economy of expression is nevertheless an intellectual value. H. L. Mencken captured the heart of the matter with his signature venom. "Democracy," Mencken (1926) declared, "is a pathetic belief in the collective wisdom of individual ignorance." Social scientists write with duller pens. Still, their conclusions tend to be better grounded. It is therefore all the more discouraging that study after study has shown the strength of prejudice along with the weakness of support for civil liberties and civil rights.

You may now be expecting to read that we will show that the conventional wisdom is wrong; not at all. Though some more Menckenesque assessments of the incompetence of voters are over the top, the evidentiary record of the shallowness of voters' understanding of public affairs and democratic values is unassailable. To be unmistakably clear, not the least of our objectives is to demonstrate that Muslims are victims not merely of prejudice—that is, ill feelings—but also discrimination—that is, unfair treatment.

But if that is all there is to say, what is there left to say, other than that the best that can be hoped from ordinary citizens is that they will stay out of the way, and leave decisions of policy and principle in the hands of their betters, the politically aware and engaged? If previous research documenting the limitations of ordinary citizens is right, how can our claim that citizens withstood the pressures and temptations to demonize Muslims, and instead stood up and defended the rights of an unpopular minority at the height of a crisis, also be right?

The route we traveled to answer this question does not conform to the textbook model of science. The prescribed path is to begin with the statement of a theory, then deduce—by a sometimes more and sometimes less rigorous process—a brace of hypotheses, and then finally, at the critical moment, present the empirical findings, which curiously in social science, almost always support the hypotheses. Of course, everyone knows that this is not the way that work is actually done. Research is invariably herky-jerky, typically kick-started by an intuition, sustained by preliminary results, and followed by a campaign of research advances, detours, and outright defeats, only to culminate (sometimes only near the end) in a coherent organization of ideas and evidence.

The analogy to a military campaign is more apt than it may seem at first sight. The presentation of research corresponds to the practice of it much the way a military historian's God's-eye account of a battle corresponds to the fog of actual war. It is not precisely that the former is a falsification of the latter. Then again, the presentational style of neither the military historian nor the social scientist is a true-to-the-facts tumult of a battle or the research process.

Why are we saying publicly what everyone knows privately? We are doing so in order to give a deservedly self-deprecating introduction to the most striking result of our study. Every study of which we are aware has shown that there is an overflow of suspicion, resentment, and hostility in western Europe toward Muslim immigrants. And every theory of prejudice of which we are aware predicts that the fear, anger, and desire for retribution that so many now feel toward Islamic fundamentalists will spill over and undercut support for the rights of Muslims. Yet our study has uncovered striking evidence of a solid defense of the rights of Muslims.

It would be pleasant to pass this discovery off as confirmation of a hypothesis we had formulated ex ante. But we are not quite entitled to receive congratulation. On the one hand, we had not elaborated a principled basis for a prediction that ordinary citizens would draw a sharp distinction between Muslims and Islamic fundamentalists. On the other hand, the whole point of the key experiment in our study was to allow for the possibility that they would treat Muslims and Islamic fundamentalists differently.[6] We thus owe our most arresting result to the nineteenth-century logician William Whewell's understanding of a hypothesis: a "happy guess." Thanks to the power of randomization,

---

[6] In the experiments, respondents are randomly assigned to distinct treatment conditions. Some are asked to make judgments about the rights of Muslims, and others about those of Islamic fundamentalists. For a detailed description of the group categorization experiment, see chapter 2.

we have confidence in the happy guess that produced far and away the most important outcome of this study: At the height of a political firestorm over cartoons satirizing the prophet Mohammed, with Muslims by the hundreds of thousands demonstrating in the streets, their country's embassy being burned, Middle Eastern governments demanding that their government apologize and ensure that nothing similar happens in the future, a decisive majority of ordinary citizens defended the civil liberties and civil rights of Muslims. It was in specifying a mechanism that would account for this noteworthy result that we reasoned our way to the principal ideas of our account. Three of these deserve special emphasis.

The first has to do with the role of categorization in political judgments. Ordinary citizens deal with the complexity of deciding the rights of controversial groups by making use of a simple rule. We spell out the mechanics of this rule in the empirical analysis. Here we want to stress that this rule is both simple and reality-oriented. Thanks to both of these properties, its application can be widely agreed on. And applying this specific rule has the quite extraordinary effect of highlighting equal support for the civil liberties of Muslim immigrants and indisputably legitimate groups in Danish politics like born-again Christians.

The second idea underpinning our account is the notion of opposing forces. Previous research has rightly focused on intolerance. How far is prejudice driving the political choices that the majority makes about issues that bear on minorities? Is it as widespread as ever or is it possibly decreasing? Where does it have its strongest hold on the electorate and where is its grasp the weakest? These are all questions that demand and deserve the attention that they have received. But the answers add up to a story about only one of the set of forces at work: those working for the exclusion of minorities. It is our hypothesis that there is an opposing set of forces: the values of liberal democracy. We will concentrate on only one of these values: tolerance.

Focusing on tolerance will seem an odd choice, since it conventionally is taken to mean no more than a willingness to put up with those one disagrees with or dislikes.[7] In contrast, we will argue for the

---

[7] There is manifestly much to recommend this conception of tolerance. For a philosophical justification, see Scanlon 2003; Williams 2005.

recovery of an older understanding of tolerance. In this older under-standing, tolerance is positive, affirmative, and supportive; it means to nourish, sustain, and succor. Operationally, what does this require? Thinking well of Muslim immigrants is insufficient. Treating them well is required. And what exactly does treating them well mean? It means the inclusion of Muslim immigrants as full members of a common com-munity entitled not only to exercise all the political rights of any other community member but also to receive all the benefits of the welfare state *without their having to sacrifice their identity as Muslims.* Since the inclusion of minorities as full members of a common community is our criterion, we will call this form of tolerance *inclusive tolerance·*

It is by bringing out the importance of inclusive tolerance in the contemporary ethos of liberal democracy that we aim to open up for discussion and further investigation of the hypothesis that the politics of minorities is a politics of opposing forces—those long recognized as working for exclusion, with intolerance chief among them—but also those yet to be properly taken into account, with the values of liberal democracy chief among them.

The third idea we center on is the paradoxical ethos of liberal de-mocracy. Thus, the most striking result of our study—a solid wall of support for the rights of Muslims at the height of the Cartoon Crisis—is testimony to the strength of liberal democracy. But a major theme of our study is that some of the strengths of democratic values, contrary to received opinion, entail weaknesses.

There are two paradoxes in particular that we will bring out. The first is that the same rule of judgment in categorizing groups that helps provide necessary protection of the civil rights of Muslims strips Is-lamic fundamentalists of the protection necessary for their civil rights. The second is that the moral covenant that underpins the welfare state simultaneously promotes equal treatment for some immigrants and opens the door to discrimination against others.

What, then, is our farthest-reaching claim? The well-documented weaknesses of citizens have obscured their strengths. That is part one, but there is also a part two. Their strengths, life being what it is, inevi-tably entail not yet appreciated weaknesses.

CHAPTER 2

A Clash of Rights

Here is the plotline of a political drama. A newspaper in a western European country, Denmark, has published a set of cartoons offensive to many Muslims. Middle Eastern governments publicly demand that the country's government apologize for the cartoons. In response, the prime minister of the western European country declares: no apology; no punishment of the newspaper for publishing the cartoons; no restrictions on future publications; no discussion.

Political leaders in the Middle East and Denmark square off. They assume the role of duelists each defending the honor of their side's values. Governments famous for their opposition to anything they see as foreign interference in their intrinsic affairs demand the right to intervene in the affairs of another country. The prime minister of a country committed to the principle of free speech vetoes any meeting with representatives of other countries who want to speak to him about the issue—and this is an especially neat twist—on the grounds that he is unconditionally committed to freedom of speech. Political leaders on both sides swear their fidelity to the highest principles. All play roles, we may be forgiven for observing, that coincide with their political self-interest—perhaps a happy coincidence, perhaps not. No doubt, politicians have principles. Then again, there is no doubt that politicians on all sides are stirring the pot to their advantage.

Then the pot boils over. Mass protests are held in Muslim countries. A Danish embassy is set ablaze. Imams issue fatwas calling for the assassination of the cartoonists. Boycotts are launched against Danish companies and products. On the other side, there are the answering volleys of Danish protest led by the prime minister himself; an avalanche of editorials and arguments urging uncompromising defense of a

foundational value of democratic politics, freedom of speech; and naturally, politician after politician queuing up to denounce interference by
foreign governments cn behalf of, of all things, a foreign religion.

This all creates a witch's brew composed of each side demanding
that its values take priority over the others, aggrieved Muslim countries insistent on a Danish apology, Danes angry in turn at the inter-
vention of Muslim countries and their insistence on a Danish apology,
and inside Denmark, Muslim imams—only a few in number, we want
to make plain, but regrettably those dominating media attention—
denouncing Danish values in the name of Islam.[1] Yet we will demonstrate that Danes impressively lined up in support of the civil rights of
Muslims. Our task is therefore a doubly unusual one: first, to show that
what informed opinion, not to mention common sense, says should
happen, did not happen, and then, to explain why what should have
happened, did not happen.

This book is a study of the crisis and thus necessarily a study of
Denmark alone. So to set our analysis in context, we begin by comparing and contrasting attitudes toward immigrants in Denmark with
those toward them in comparable countries. Then we turn to the all-
important question, Did the fear and anger that Danes almost uni-
versally felt toward Islamic fundamentalists spill over and undercut
support for the civil rights of Muslims?

How could Muslims escape being scapegoats for the acts of Islamic
terrorists? That seems almost a rhetorical question. It was not just the
years of terror and immediate threat of Islamic terror. There was also
the flame-throwing rhetoric of some Danes acting, wittingly or not, as
political provocateurs. One example should suffice. "There are only two
possible reactions if we want to stop this bomb terror," radio host Kaj
Vilhelmsen declared: "either to drive away all foreign Mohammedans
from western Europe so that they cannot place bombs, or to extermi-
nate the fanatic Mohammedans, that are still a large part of the Mohammedan immigrants. But if the governments and the authorities do
not want to react to the Mohammedan terror and crush it with power,
then the citizens have to do it themselves."[2]

---

[1] As mentioned below, however, the situation also prompted the formation of an organization called "Democratic Muslims" as a counterweight to the more radical imams.

[2] Quoted in Bech Thomsen 2006, 22.

The task of this chapter is to explain why, even in the cauldron of a crisis over the claims of Islam, fear of and anger toward Islamic fundamentalists did not spill over to Muslims in Denmark. Our specific concern is the support for the civil rights of Danish Muslims. Our strategy is to abstract away from the details of the crisis as well as Danish politics. Instead, we will advance a theory of group categorization and civil rights.

Our theoretical premise is that it is not possible to form individualized judgments about the civil rights to which each and every group is entitled. It is not possible for ordinary citizens or, for that matter, political theorists. All of us must simplify, and we simplify by organizing groups into a small number of categories—indeed, as an empirical matter, into two categories. Muslims are assigned to one category, and Islamic fundamentalists are assigned to a quite different one. We are not suggesting that the two, to borrow a metaphor, are assigned to separate watertight compartments. But we mean to show that ordinary citizens drew a clear distinction between them. The public at large—routinely derided as so ill informed about politics and incoherent in their thinking as to be unable to discharge the duties of democratic citizenship—in fact treated Muslims as they would treat groups that are controversial but undeniably legitimate. Ours, then, is a story of ordinary citizens keeping their moral balance throughout the crisis, from its height to its end.

HOSTILITY TOWARD IMMIGRANTS: A COMPARATIVE PERSPECTIVE

Every country is like every other in at least one way. Every country is also unlike every other, almost always in more than one way. For our story, the way that counts more than any other is how similar—or dissimilar—Denmark is to other western European countries in its fears about foreign immigrants. Are Danes, perhaps, more hostile, and less ready to accept immigrants? Or are they more accommodating, and less ready to reject them? Or yet again, are they more or less like citizens elsewhere, neither more inclusive nor more intolerant?

The European Social Survey affords a panoramic view of popular attitudes toward immigrants in western Europe. The survey administers a common questionnaire to representative samples of citizens, in an array of countries, on a regular basis. Among the areas it investigates are attitudes toward immigrants. The focus of our study is the reactions of Danes to the crisis. So it is necessary to see if their attitudes were much like—or quite unlike—citizens elsewhere in western Europe before the crisis. Accordingly, table 2.1 presents an overview of attitudes toward immigrants in six countries: Denmark, Germany, France, the United Kingdom, the Netherlands, and Sweden.

Sweden stands out. Time after time, it shows itself to be the most tolerant country. The differences between Sweden and the other countries are not always large, but they are consistent. The most eye-popping example is opposition to the idea that "if a country wants to reduce tensions, it should stop immigration." Support for raising the drawbridges to bring immigration to a stop is at least twice and more often three times larger in all the other countries than it is in Sweden. In Denmark, for instance, 47 percent agree with the proposition that "if a country wants to reduce tensions, it should stop immigration"; in Sweden, in contrast, only 16 percent agree. Other indicators in table 2.1 point in the same direction. Swedes are the most open to cultural diversity, the least in favor of residential segregation, and the least opposed to intermarriages with immigrants. All in all, if it is an exaggeration to speak of Swedish exceptionalism, it is a pardonable one.

Sweden aside, the striking feature of table 2.1 is the pattern of similarity overall across countries. One country is more tolerant according to one indicator, another country is more tolerant according to a different indicator, and still another country is more tolerant by yet another indicator. Consider attitudes about whether immigrants who commit a serious crime should be deported. Eight in ten in Denmark agree that these immigrants should be deported. For all intents and purposes, the balance of opinion is the same in the United Kingdom, the Netherlands, and for that matter Sweden. Support for deportation is even higher in Germany, however—on the order of nine in ten in favor of evicting immigrants convicted of a serious crime.

A stereotype leaps to mind: Deutschland über alles. But the other results in table 2.1 make plain why that when drawing conclusions, caution trumps speed. Look at the reactions to the question of whether "it is better for a country if almost everyone shares the same customs

TABLE 2.1 Immigrant Attitudes in Denmark, Germany, France, the United Kingdom, the Netherlands, and Sweden (Percent Intolerant Responses)

	DK	D	F	UK	NL	S
If immigrants commit a serious crime, they should be made to leave (strongly agree + agree).	80	91	67	79	76	75
It is better for a country if almost everyone shares the same customs and traditions (strongly agree + agree).	46	39	54	46	44	37
If a country wants to reduce tensions, it should stop immigration (strongly agree + agree).	47	47	34	44	37	16
Preferring to live in an area where almost nobody was of a different race or ethnic group from most [nationals of country] (rather than in areas where some people were of a different race or ethnic group from most [nationals of country], or many people were of a different race or ethnic group).	37	24	23	26	32	20
Most people who come to live here work and pay taxes. They also use health and welfare services. On average, do you think people who come here take out more than they put in or put in more than they take out? Scores 0–4 on 0 (generally take out more) to 10 (generally put in more) scale.	53	56	41	56	47	40
Would you say it is generally bad or good for [country's] economy that people come to live here from other countries? Scores 0–4 on 0 (bad for the economy) to 10 (good for the economy) scale.	41	31	28	44	34	27
Are [country's] crime problems made worse or better by immigrants? Scores 0–4 on 0 (crime problems made worse) to 10 (crime problems made better) scale.	70	76	60	61	81	69
And now thinking of immigrants who are of a different race or ethnic group from most [nationals of country], how much would you mind or not mind if someone like this married a close relative of yours? Scores 6–10 on 0 (not mind at all) to 10 (mind a lot) scale.	32	23	30	23	26	17

Source: European Social Survey, round 1, 2002.

Note: DK: Denmark (N: 1,362–1,456); D: Germany (N: 2,797–2,909); F: France (1,475–1,494); UK: United Kingdom (N: 1,995–2,043); NL: Netherlands (N: 2,288–2,354); S: Sweden (N: 1,880–1,963).

and traditions." Germany ties with Sweden for the lowest level of agreement. Denmark, the Netherlands, and the United Kingdom fall in the middle of the pack, while France displays the highest level of agreement with the principle of cultural homogeneity. Yet again it pays to look before leaping. France is second only to Sweden (and not by much) in rejecting the proposition that immigrants take more than they contribute to society. In sum, according to some criteria one country is more tolerant than the others, though usually by a small margin, but according to other criteria, a different country is more tolerant, again by a small margin.

How, then, should Denmark be characterized? In some respects, opinion about immigrants is more negative in Denmark than in most other countries, as indicated by, for example, the belief that immigration is bad for the economy, the opposition to intermarriage with immigrants, and support for racial integration. More often, though, the balance of opinion in Denmark seems in line with that of other countries, such as in perceptions of immigrants as welfare exploiters or opposition to multiculturalism. All in all, our judgment is that Denmark tends to score toward the higher end of opposition to immigrants, but not markedly or distinctively more so than comparable countries.

ISLAMOPHOBIA AND THE "CATEGORIZATION" HYPOTHESIS

What drove the Cartoon Crisis? Muslims—or to be more precise, their self-appointed spokesmen and Middle Eastern governments—demanded that freedom of expression take second place to the prevention of blasphemy and mocking of Islam. How did Danes see their demands? Common sense would suggest that to ask this question is to answer it. Muslims are demanding that "their" values take priority over "ours." To add insult to injury, "we" must apologize to "them." Considering the levels of suspicion and resentment against immigrants shown in table 2.1 three years before the crisis, was a reaction against Muslims in Denmark not inevitable?

The answer is surely yes, according to informed opinion. Dread and dislike of Muslims, it is agreed, "have existed in western countries and culture for several centuries. In the last twenty years," expert opinion holds that "the dislike has become more explicit, more extreme and more dangerous. It is an ingredient of all sections of our media and is prevalent in all sections of our society. Within Britain [and presumptively, western Europe generally] it means that Muslims are frequently excluded from the economic, social and public life of the nation . . . and are frequently victims of discrimination and harassment."[3]

Spillover is the metaphor: "dread or hatred of Islam and therefore, fear and dislike of all Muslims."[4] The last two decades have seen large-scale bombings, attempted bombings, and assassinations in England, Spain, Germany, and France, among other countries, and—immediately relevant for us—Denmark as well. It would be understandable, albeit regrettable, under these circumstances that Islamic radicalism and Muslims have become closely coupled in the minds of the ordinary citizen—so closely that when many see one, they see the other.

How could it be otherwise? Radical imams have become the public face of Islamic fundamentalism. They denounce Western society and its values. A liberal society, they preach, is an incitement to abandon the ways of the true faith; its open and relentless advertisement of sexuality is an abomination; and its failure to condemn Israel and support the cause of Palestine are proof of its implacable hostility to Islam. Islamic fundamentalists do not speak for all Muslims, it should be unnecessary to say, but their voices are the loudest. When Danish citizens hear imams justify bombings or assassination attempts, how can they not feel that Islamic radicals are a threat to their safety and way of life? And could their fear and anger at Islamic radicals not spill over into resentment and rejection of Muslims in Denmark?

Islamophobia is contagious. "Dread or hatred of Islam" spills over into "fear and dislike of all Muslims."[5] And here common sense is supported by the results of both quantitative and qualitative research. The "spill over" hypothesis follows directly from the core concept of ethnocentrism—that is, the tendency for the dislike and disdain of one out-group to be correlated with the dislike and disdain of others.[6]

[3] Runnymede Trust 1997, 1.

[4] For a qualitative analysis of the reactions of young Muslims to the connection between terror and Islam, see Mythen, Walklate, and Khan 2009. For a quantitatively grounded study, see Hussain and Miller 2006.

[5] Runneymede Trust 1997, 1.

[6] See the discussion in Kinder and Kam 2009.

Moreover, researchers deeply informed by the study of other countries' history and culture contend that the spill over hypothesis holds, possibly with special force, for Danes. Commenting on reactions to the assassination of Theo van Gogh in 2004, Gilles Kepel, a political analyst noted for his sensitivity to complexity and context, judged that the murder "struck an even deeper chord of fear and distrust in the Danish population [than in the Dutch]." "A number of Danes," Kepel (2008, 219) went on to observe, "began to think of Muslims as religious fanatics who abused political asylum, engaged in nefarious activities such as drug trafficking, and sometimes conspired to commit heinous crimes."

Civil Rights and the Categorization of Groups

Our concern is with the support for the rights of democratic citizenship for minority groups in western Europe. The plural noun *groups* dominates the adjective *different*. Experts as well as citizens at large cannot formulate a separate judgment of the rights of each and every social and political group. There are simply too many, far too many, to make and remember individualized judgments about each. Reducing the number of them by remarking similarities among them is the way out. In short, categorization is necessary.[7]

In making judgments about political rights, it is our hypothesis that citizens make use of two distinct categories.[8] One category is groups whose views are at odds with those of the larger society. Typically, they present a critique of society or the economy. They wish society to be different, and not by a small degree but fundamentally. They are in the business of advocating change, often loudly, and sometimes dramatically. But they are not attempting or threatening to achieve change by force. We label groups like this as "out of the mainstream."

A second category of groups does not aim simply at persuading or cajoling their fellow citizens to see the larger society as they do. Nor are they willing to settle for the larger society tolerating their views.

[7] For the classic study, see Rosch and Mervis 1975. We are following the specific lead of Stephen Nicholson and his collaborators. See Heit and Nicholson 2010; Nicholson et al. 2011.

[8] For altogether obvious reasons, we are excluding from consideration groups whose claim to rights is uncontroversial.

They are adversaries, not just critics. They have aggressively pitted themselves against the larger society. Membership in these groups is not, in and of itself, against the law. Yet members of them have a record of going beyond the limits of the law or moral norms. Accordingly, we refer to these groups as "transgressive."

How does the distinction between out-of-the-mainstream and transgressive categories map onto the categorization of Muslims and Islamic fundamentalists? The issues raised by the Muslim community in Denmark have been low-voltage ones, such as halal food in kindergartens or the establishment of separate showers for Muslim children in connection with physical education classes in schools. Most of these concerns were easy to meet and indeed have been met. Nor should the conduct of the largest number of Danish Muslims in response to the publication of the cartoons be neglected. A small demonstration in Copenhagen, a few press releases and emails, and a call for a "sleep-in" and strike that was ignored hardly constitute a firestorm of reaction within Denmark.[9] For that matter, during the crisis itself, a then-prominent member of the Social Liberal Party, Naser Khader, who is of Syrian origin, founded the organization Democratic Muslims to promote the idea that Islam is reconcilable with democracy. Yes, Muslims in Denmark excite controversy. But no, they have not as a community pitted themselves against the larger society.

In contrast, consider the record of Islamic fundamentalists in Denmark. The most prominent group of Islamic fundamentalists is the Danish branch of the international organization Hizb ut Tahrir. Its avowed aim is to abolish democracy in favor of a caliphate.[10] Hizb ut Tahrir's leader has been convicted of racism for anti-Semitic statements. The group also has a reputation for being a sect and leaning hard on members wanting to leave the organization. During the Cartoon Crisis, leading figures of the Copenhagen-based organization Islamisk Trossamfund won media exposure by taking part in a delegation traveling to the Middle East to whip up popular anger. Subsequent terrorist plots

---

[9] Jytte Klausen (2009, 87) notes the irony that the imams circulated the cartoons they regarded as blasphemous to the Muslim community in Denmark in order to mobilize it.

[10] That is, an autocracy with a religious leader.

have cemented the reputation of Islamic fundamentalists as transgressive radicals.[11]

The boundary between the two categories—out of the mainstream, on one side of the line, and transgressive, on the other—is thus grounded in behavior. This conceptualization, though not precisely the same, follows the spirit of the distinction between democratic and antidemocratic groups that John Sullivan and his colleagues drew in their seminal study of political tolerance, apart from our emphasis on actual behavior.[12] Transgressive groups have a reputation for violating legal or moral limits of society.

The phrase "reputation for violating" should sound an alarm for anyone committed to freedom of thought and expression. To say that a group is associated with violence is not to assert that many, let alone most, of its members have broken or will break the law. To say that Islamic terrorists are Islamic fundamentalists is not to maintain that many, let alone most, Islamic fundamentalists are terrorists. But the record of Islamic terror attacks is real. So, too, is the assaultive rhetoric of the most visible—because most provocative—imams. And the consequence, we hypothesize, is that Muslims and Islamic fundamentalists are placed in different categories. Citizens will draw a sharp distinction between the claims to political rights of the two groups.[13] It is not merely that they will give more support to Muslims than to Islamic fundamentalists. It is that the difference between the levels of support

[11] The first decade of the twenty-first century has also seen a number of court cases against alleged terrorists, all of whom have been apprehended before they could carry out any attacks. Three cases have concerned actual plans to carry out a terrorist act, and two of them led to convictions (in one case with sentences of up to twelve years in prison). A fourth case led to the conviction of a fairly prominent Islamist publisher for providing assistance to al-Qaida in the form, for instance, of materials to be used for recruiting new terrorists. The publisher—known in Denmark as "the bookseller from Brønshøj"—has previously been involved in court cases, and due also to his contacts to radical Islamists abroad, has therefore attracted some media interest. His presence in Denmark is the perhaps most prominent example of the mind-set that prevailed pre-9/11. Thus, his views and contacts have been known for quite some years, but particularly in the early 1990s, he was allowed to go about his business without any interference by the authorities.

[12] Sullivan, Pierson, and Marcus 1982. See also Petersen et al. 2010a.

[13] The literature on political tolerance toward different groups is voluminous; as such, we cannot cite it all. For core contributions, however, see Gibson 1998, 2006; Gibson and Gouws 2003; Mondak and Sanders 2003; Rohrschneider 1996; Sniderman et al. 1989, 1996.

for the rights of the two groups will be so large as to approximate a difference in kind, not merely degree. We call this the categorization hypothesis.[14]

PUBLIC SUPPORT FOR POLITICAL RIGHTS: MUSLIMS VERSUS ISLAMIC FUNDAMENTALISTS

To assess levels of support for the political rights of a variety of groups, we conducted a group categorization experiment. Here is how the experiment works: respondents are asked whether a group is entitled to have a certain set of political rights, and the particular group they are asked about is decided on a random basis. Two of the groups that we asked about were Muslims and Islamic fundamentalists.

Political rights differ in standing. Some rights are integral to liberal democracy and therefore less readily contestable. Others are more peripheral and thus more readily contestable. Our strategy, accordingly, is to investigate support for both integral and peripheral political rights. Two integral rights are the right to take part in public debate and the right to demonstrate. Two more peripheral rights are the "right" to speak in high schools and the right to privacy. The respondents were asked about each of these rights. The wording of the questions was always the same. The order of the questions was also always the same. But crucially, as mentioned above, the group that they were asked about was decided on a purely random basis.

Three points about this design deserve underlining. First, thanks to the experimental randomization, the respondents asked about Muslims are like the respondents asked about Islamic fundamentalists in every respect, chance differences aside. Second, the respondents asked about Muslims had no way of knowing that the other respondents were being asked about Islamic fundamentalists, and vice versa. And third, since they were asked about one or the other group but not

---

[14] We hasten to add that although we cannot, due to data limitations, show that the two categories—transgressive and out of the mainstream—are exhaustive in the sense that all controversial groups can be placed in either, we do in fact believe them to be. Hence, our conjecture is that they form a set of natural categories. It is the task of subsequent research that uses an encompassing list of groups, however, to show that this is indeed so.

TABLE 2.2 Support for Civil Rights of Muslims and Islamic Fundamentalists
(Percent)

	Debate	Demonstrate	Speak at high schools	Oppose telephone tapping
Muslims	71	81	74	51
Islamic fundamentalists	51	61	44	18

Note: N varies from 466 to 503. The standard errors of the entries vary from 1.7 to 2.3.
Question wording: 1. Representatives for [group] should not be allowed to express themselves in public debate; 2. The police should have better opportunities for tapping telephones owned by [group]; 3. Representatives for [group] should have the right to speak at high schools; 4. Also [group] should be allowed to hold demonstrations. The response categories were: completely agree, somewhat agree, neither agree nor disagree, somewhat disagree, completely disagree, or don't know. Entries are the sums of completely and somewhat disagree responses for the debate and wiretap items, and completely and somewhat agree for the right to speak at high schools and demonstration items.

both, the views they expressed about one group could not influence the views they expressed about the other.

Table 2.2 shows the levels of public support for civil rights for Muslims and Islamic fundamentalists. Consider the reactions to the two fundamental rights: the right to take part in public debate and the right to demonstrate.[15] Seventy-one percent support the right of Muslims to take part in public debates; only 51 percent support the right of Islamic fundamentalists to do so. The same pattern applies to the right to protest. Eighty-one percent support the right of the former to demonstrate; just 61 percent support the right of the latter to do so. In short, consistent with the categorization hypothesis, ordinary citizens draw a clear distinction between Muslims and Islamic fundamentalists even on civil rights integral to democratic politics.

And they draw an even sharper distinction when it comes to more peripheral civil rights. As the third column of table 2.2 shows, 74 percent support the right of Muslims to address high school students, compared to only 44 percent willing to welcome Islamic fundamentalists into the classroom. To be sure, to speak of a right to speak at a school will sound, to non-Danish ears, like a misuse of the concept

[15] As is clear from table 2.2, three of the rights items are phrased in the positive, while the debate item is phrased in the negative. The figures in the table represent, for all four items, the percentage of tolerant responses.

of rights. What is at issue is not whether any and all persons should have the right to demand to address high school students but rather whether or not specific groups should a priori be excluded from being invited to address high school students if the principal or a teacher at the school should wish to extend such an invitation. The question, naturally, arises as to why anyone would wish to invite contentious groups to speak at a high school. The answer lies in the openness of the Danish democratic tradition. It is quite common for high schools to invite members of minority groups and/or parties to talk to the students in order to broaden their horizons as well as introduce them to different views in society. A gaudily notorious example illuminates the practice. In the 1990s, a leader of the Danish Hell's Angels gave several talks at high schools. He did so before a subsequent gang war broke out, it is true. Then again, he gave his talk while on leave from prison, where he was serving his sixteen-year sentence for the murder of a rival biker president. If a person who is an acknowledged gang leader and convicted murderer may be invited to give a talk to high school students, others may reasonably presume they should be allowed to do so, too.

Finally, consider the reactions to a proposal to enlarge the authority of the police to engage in wiretapping (the fourth column of table 2.2). Danish law has permitted wiretapping for a long time, and indeed the parliament has broadened the police's authority to tap telephones as part of the post-9/11 antiterrorism measures.[16] Approving of wiretapping, it follows, is not in and of itself evidence of opposition to the civil rights of a particular person or group. But previous research has also shown that a readiness to approve of wiretaps tends to go along with a readiness to approve of limitations on civil rights.[17] Approval of wiretapping is thus an indicator—albeit a systematically ambiguous one—of a lack of support for political rights. Granting the ambiguity, we ourselves are struck by the magnitude of difference between the levels of opposition to wiretapping Muslims versus wiretapping Islamic fundamentalists. While 51 percent are opposed to the police having

[16] One example of the contents of the new law is that police were given the ability to obtain court orders pertaining to tapping all phone calls from a given individual rather than tapping only specific telephone numbers.

[17] Sniderman et al. 1996, 26–36.

broader power to wiretap Muslims, in contrast, only 18 percent oppose it for Islamic fundamentalists.

What, then, do these initial results from the group categorization experiment show? A crisis—the most serious since World War II, the prime minister declared—had erupted. No one could be ignorant of it. No one could ignore it. If they did not bring it up in conversations with friends, family, or coworkers, friends, family, or coworkers would bring it up for them. No Dane had experienced anything like the international political backlash against Denmark; governments in the Middle East furiously protested, while others enjoyed the pleasures of self-righteousness—a memorable instance being Bill Clinton's declaration, "None of us are totally free of stereotypes about people of different races, different ethnic groups, and different religions. . . . [T]here [is] this appalling example in Northern Europe, in Denmark . . . these totally outrageous cartoons against Islam."[18] Notwithstanding this storm of criticism, Danes kept their political balance. They drew a clear line between Muslims and Islamic fundamentalists. Decisive majorities stood up for the civil rights of Muslims in Denmark, with the exception only of wiretapping.[19]

We believe that these are important results. Islamophobia has become a fashionable concept—almost a branding strategy to advertise a specialized form of prejudice.[20] Anger toward and resentment of Islamic fundamentalists must spill over and color feelings about Muslims to some degree. Nonetheless, the fact of the matter is that Danes reacted quite differently to Muslims and Islamic fundamentalists, as our results indicated, as though they belong to two quite different and distinct categories of groups.

This carries us some distance, but not across the goal line. To observe that Danes gave more support to the rights of Muslims than they

---

[18] Clinton was speaking at an economic conference in Doha on January 30, 2006; see *Jyllands-Posten*, January 31, 2006, section 1, page 6. The quote was distributed worldwide by Agence France-Presse.

[19] Superficially, our results may appear at odds with other research. So we have scrutinized the leading work: Davis 2007; Kalkan, Layman, and Ushlaner 2009; Merolla and Zechmeister 2009; Brooks and Manza 2013. In fact, the disjunction in responses to Muslims and Islamic fundamentalists is consistent with the conclusions of all studies that primarily focus on transgressive groups.

[20] Runnymede Trust 1997, 1.

did to those of Islamic fundamentalists is not evidence that they treated Muslims well.

The Distinctness of Category Boundaries

The first part of the categorization hypothesis holds that citizens assign controversial groups to two distinct and different categories: out-of-the-mainstream groups—that is, groups whose views are at odds with those of the larger society, but nonetheless manifestly have a legitimate place in it—and transgressive groups—groups that are not merely critical or out of step with the society but also actively pit themselves against it. A second prediction thus follows from the categorization hypothesis: not only are Muslims and Islamic fundamentalists treated differently, Muslims are treated as well as Danish groups that may be contentious but are indisputably legitimate.

What is the ideal group to test this prediction? It is Christian fundamentalists, or as they are more commonly called in Denmark, born-again Christians. This may surprise those unfamiliar with contemporary Danish life—and perhaps some who are familiar. By law, Denmark is a religious society. Its constitution, while guaranteeing freedom of religion, stipulates that the Protestant Lutheran Church is the state church. The monarch is the head of it. Far and away most Danes are members of this church, even though this requires them to pay an extra tax of about 1 percent of their income.[21] All this gives the appearance of a dedicated Christian country. But appearance is what this is. Typically, Danes attend church only for ceremonial events and Christmas, while the last half century or so has seen a profound liberalization of social norms regarding abortion, pornography, and couples living together and having children out of wedlock, among many other things. Denmark has become a secular society through and through.

It is, however, one of the more piquant ironies that a commitment to a secular society invigorates religious traditionalists. Precisely in response to the secularity of modern Denmark, born-again Christians, often organized in so-called *frikirker*—that is, free churches existing

---

[21] The number is 81.5 percent, according to Statistics Denmark (www.statistikbanken.dk, table KM1).

outside the state church—are fighting to restore the old values and way of life. This strain of Christianity is deeply moralistic and restrictive. It has fought tough as nails against the liberalization of the larger society, above all on issues of abortion, pornography, and homosexuality. In the thoroughly secular society of contemporary Denmark, born-again Christians are an out-of-the-mainstream group. Yet they indisputably have a legitimate place in Danish society. How indisputably? Under Danish law, they may establish their own schools and receive public funding for them.[22]

Other examples of out-of-the-mainstream groups are the far Left and far Right in politics. Both denounce contemporary society as unjust, albeit from diametrically opposing standpoints. Both the far Left and far Right are advocates for radical changes to the status quo, albeit in diametrically opposing directions. It is one thing to advocate radical change, though. It is quite another to throw oneself in opposition to the society, reject its rules, challenge its jurisdiction, and violate the limits of its laws. To be sure, tiny groups at both ideological extremes are willing to breach accepted boundaries. But these minute factions aside, the far Left and far Right are active participants in Danish politics, competing in every election for the support of voters. They are deeply critical of the values and practices of contemporary society. Yet they make their case accepting its rules. Born-again Christians along with the far Left and far Right thereby fall in a common category. If our reasoning is right, then Muslims do too.

What groups are similar to Islamic fundamentalists? Transgressive groups pit themselves against society. They are adversaries, not advocates. Their members regularly break the moral norms and sometimes the legal ones as well. Bikers in Denmark are a window display example. Think of Hell's Angels but add two things. They deploy a larger arsenal, including armor-piercing rockets as well as bombs, and operate on a smaller stage They thus enjoy—if that is the right word—a

---

[22] Under the rules regulating *friskoler*, these schools' budgets are 75 percent publicly funded, even though they operate outside the public system and have wide discretion regarding their curriculum. Nonetheless, Christian schools modeling their curriculum after born-again Christian schools in the United States have provoked controversy for failing to meet curriculum requirements and teaching standards, and at least one such school has had its funding removed. This is not a right restricted to born-again Christians, it should be emphasized. Muslims in Denmark, for example, qualify too.

prominence in Denmark that, for instance, their counterparts in the United States do not.

Another example of a transgressive group is the Autonome, a Danish contribution to the list of quasi-revolutionary leftist groups found all over western Europe. As the name suggests, the Autonome is a loose grouping of anarchist youths. Like anarchists in other countries, they demonstrate and stage happenings, but that does not always satisfy their spleen. In 2007, for example, the Autonome engaged in battle with the authorities over their fortified headquarters in Copenhagen. The streets of Copenhagen were turned into a war zone of burning cars and looted shops for a number of days. A final case of a transgressive group is neo-Nazis. While neo-Nazi groups are politically impotent in contemporary Danish politics, this does not lessen the fact that they are morally transgressive.[23] They have chosen to identify themselves explicitly with a movement that broke all bounds of morality and humanity, and their links with football hooligans certainly don't help their image.

A premise of the categorization hypothesis is that "like" are seen as alike. It follows that just as Muslims and born-again Christians should be seen as like, Islamic fundamentalists and bikers, the Autonome, or even neo-Nazis should be seen as alike. If both are not true, then the categorization hypothesis is not true. We therefore commissioned a study to test this prediction on a data set separate from the one that suggested it.[24]

A representative sample of the Danish general population was asked to rate a number of groups on their respect for democracy and propensity for violence.[25] These two attributes track the distinction that we have drawn between groups that are contentious but legitimate and those that are transgressive. Following what is our standard practice,

---

[23] On occasion, they have run for municipal elections in a community, but have received only a few votes.

[24] The group categorization study was conducted as a web survey by the Zapera polling agency in December 2008. The respondents were recruited from eighteen- to seventy-year-olds in Zapera's standing so-called Denmark Panel. Out of the 2,766 respondents contacted, answers were obtained from 1,023 people, yielding a response rate (AAPOR RR1) of 37 percent. The data were subsequently weighted for gender, age, and region of residence to conform to the relevant population. Details on the representativeness of the survey are available in the online appendix (http://press.princeton.edu/titles/10400.html).

[25] For the wording of the questions, see figure 2.1.

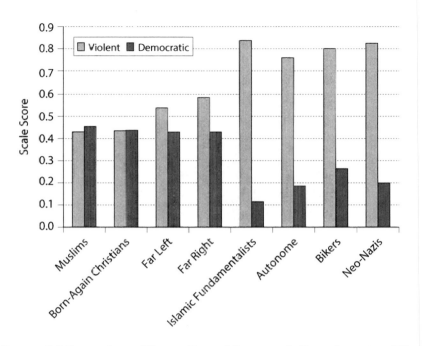

FIGURE 2.1 Perceptions of Target Groups' Democratic Commitment and Use of Violence (Scale Scores)

Note: N varies from 890 to 997. Standard errors vary from 0.006 to 0.01. Question wording: [Violent:] "Here is a list of groups in Denmark. For each group please indicate how *violent* you think the group is." The scale ran from "0 not at all violent" to "10 very violent." The answers were rescaled to run from 0 to 1. [Democratic:] "Here is a list of groups in Denmark. For each group please indicate whether you think the group *respects the rules of democracy*." The scale ran from "0 does not at all respect the rules of democracy" to "10 completely respects the rules of democracy." The answers were rescaled to run from 0 to 1. Both items also included "don't know" options.

the scale used for measuring Danes' perceptions has 11 points, and has been rescored to run from 0 to 1.

Figure 2.1 presents the ratings of the eight groups. One could not hope for a more clean-cut differentiation. The groups unmistakably fall into two separate clusters. The mean score on the violence scale for the grouping on the right—Islamic fundamentalists, the Autonome, bikers, and neo-Nazis—is 0.81, while their mean rating on the respect for democracy scale is just the reverse, 0.19. By any standard, these groups are not perceived as merely out of the mainstream but instead as transgressive and out of bounds. In contrast, the four groups on the left in figure 2.1—Muslims, born-again Christians, the far Left, and the far Right—are placed near the midpoint of both scales. Their mean score on the respect for democracy scale is 0.44. Their mean score on the violence scale is 0.49. They are rated more favorably than groups on the right in the figure, though they are not rated all that favorably. They are indeed out of the mainstream.

Two points were at issue here. First, would the eight groups fall into two distinct categories? The answer is yes. Second, would Muslims and Islamic fundamentalists again be assigned to two distinctly different categories? The answer also is yes.

DISCRIMINATION OR EQUAL TREATMENT?

Figure 2.1 supplies evidence of how the groups are perceived, not how they are treated. The two are not the same. It is one thing to see Muslims as similar to born-again Christians. It is quite another to treat them the same as born-again Christians. Fortunately, the group categorization experiment was designed to determine just this.

How, then, do our respondents behave in the group categorization experiment? Specifically, do they treat Muslims the same as Danish groups that have a legitimate place in Danish life, as the categorization hypothesis predicts? Panel A of table 2.3 compares levels of support for the political rights of the out-of-the-mainstream groups—Muslims, born-again Christians, the far Left, and the far Right.

The pattern is clear-cut. Compare the responses toward Muslims and born-again Christians: 81 percent support the right of the former to demonstrate, compared to 83 percent for the latter; 71 percent support of the right of the former to take part in public debate, compared to 68 percent. The other figures tell the same story. Danes treat Muslims as they treat other controversial but legitimate groups, lining up in support of their civil rights and civil liberties, and what is more, by an overwhelming majority on three out of four of our measures.

Panel B of table 2.3 presents the level of support for the rights of Islamic fundamentalists and our three other exemplars of transgressive groups: the Autonome, bikers, and neo-Nazis. Comparing panel B to panel A, the most obvious difference is that levels of support for the

TABLE 2.3 Support for the Rights of Target Groups (Percent)

	Debate	Demonstrate	Speak at high schools	Oppose telephone tapping
Panel A: Out-of-the-Mainstream Groups				
Muslims	71	81	74	51
Born-again Christians	68	83	64	50
Far Left	76	81	72	49
Far Right	73	77	61	36
Panel B: Transgressive Groups				
Islamic fundamentalists	51	61	44	18
Autonome	71	76	48	36
Bikers	59	73	52	24
Neo-Nazis	53	59	31	24

Note: N varies from 439 to 503. The standard errors of the entries vary from 1.7 to 2.4. For question wording and details, see table 2.2.

civil rights of transgressive groups are markedly lower than for those of out-of-the-mainstream groups. Commonsensical as this is, it is reassuring all the same. Had it not been so, it would have made no sense to speak of two distinct groups.

Judging from the results of panel B, Islamic fundamentalists fall in the middle of the category of transgressive groups. On the one hand, there is more support for the right of bikers (73 percent) to demonstrate than for Islamic fundamentalists (61 percent) to do the same. On the other hand, there is more support for the right of Islamic fundamentalists to demonstrate than for neo-Nazis (59 percent) to do likewise. In only one respect do Islamic fundamentalists stand out: there is less opposition to tapping their telephones than to wiretapping those of any of the other groups. To our minds, this is no more than a commonsensical result. The more relevant point, for the analysis of civil rights in general, is that there is not a lot of opposition to wiretapping any of the other groups.

What does this add up to? Our findings are a "good" news story. Danes treat Muslims as well as fellow Danes. At the same time, they are a "bad" news story. Danes treat Islamic fundamentalists the same as they treat bikers or other groups whose members have a reputation for breaking the moral or legal norms of the larger society. Here is the first of our two paradoxes—the categorization paradox. The same rule of judgment in categorizing groups that helps provide necessary protection of the civil rights of Muslims strips Islamic fundamentalists of the protection necessary for their civil rights.

THE "JUST BELOW THE SURFACE" HYPOTHESIS

It was not unreasonable to fear that the Cartoon Crisis would trigger a backlash against Muslims, though in fact it did not.[26] It was not unreasonable because fear of a backlash is grounded not only in reality-oriented anxiety about the reactions of ordinary citizens to events since 9/11 but also in a deep concern about their underlying susceptibility to prejudice against Muslims, among many other minorities, that long predated 9/11. For a generation now, a dominant theme in social science has been the illusion of tolerance. Western democracies appear more tolerant of minorities than a half century ago. But expressions of support for tolerance, in the judgment of many social scientists, often go only skin deep.[27] They reflect not a change of feelings toward minorities but rather a change in societal norms of what it is socially acceptable (and unacceptable) to say. Under the pressure of these new norms, large numbers of ordinary citizens suppress the antipathy they still feel toward minorities or find ways to express it subtly. But their resentment, anger, and disdain toward minorities lurk just below the surface. Given the opportunity, and they are vigilant in spotting one, to express their hostility, they will seize it, and their hostility to minorities will break through their veneer of tolerance. Accordingly, we call this the just below the surface hypothesis.

This hypothesis tends to be treated as though its validity is self-evident, and for a principled reason: a deep concern about the horrific power of prejudice. It is, arguably, moral vanity to presume to rank the horrors of the long twentieth century, especially because the singular lesson of the Holocaust is that there are no limits to the evil that one group will do to another. Then, too, the distinctively US sin

---

[26] See, for example, comments by sociology professor Peter Gundelach in *Jyllands-Posten*, February 26, 2006, sec. 2, 1.

[27] For a classic study, see Jackman and Muha 1984. See also studies on symbolic racism: Kinder and and Sanders 1996; Kinder and Sears 1981.

of entrenching racial immiseration has taught a universal lesson about liberal democracy's susceptibility to violations of its own values, and no less, the barrier that these values can put up to overcoming inequality. It thus only appears to be a contradiction that progress in combating prejudice spurs an insistence on the persistence of prejudice. Fearing the ever-present risk of falling backward, and all too painfully aware of the continuing effort necessary to go forward, the best in us leads us to believe the worst of others.

Given the apparently self-evident validity of the just below the surface hypothesis, the question for those concerned about the values of liberal democracy was not whether the Cartoon Crisis would trigger a backlash against Muslims. It was how far-reaching that backlash would be. But we have seen that there was not a backlash. So the question becomes, Is the apparently self-evidently valid just below the surface hypothesis in fact valid?

To test the hypothesis, we take advantage of a fifteen-year sequence of public opinion surveys that included questions assessing attitudes toward immigrants. The sequence begins in 1993 and continues at tightly packed intervals.[28] Obvious though it is, it is worth saying explicitly that this sequence of studies starts before 9/11, and covers all the subsequent years in which there has been a steady stream of terrorist threats and attacks.

If the just below the surface hypothesis is correct, we will observe spikes in hostility to immigrants, perhaps after 9/11, perhaps after the first London bombing, but in any case at some point in time during this fifteen-year period of Islamic terror. For that matter, the Cartoon Crisis itself is custom-tailored to test the idea that many are just waiting for a convenient pretext to express their true feelings toward minorities. If an attack on the foundational value of freedom of expression does not qualify as a socially acceptable opportunity for the presumed prejudice

---

[28] The median time between data points is one year. In addition—and to show the generality of the results—we also include measures from the Danish National Election Study. Some questions were asked in all or nearly all of the studies. The wording of the questions, moreover, is identical over this period, as are the response formats—except for our survey, which supplies the 2006 observations, and the Danish National Election Study. Both, thus, use a neutral alternative (neither/nor) on the standard (Likert) response scale—an option that was not present in the other surveys. For comparability, we have excluded the neutral category from the percentage base.

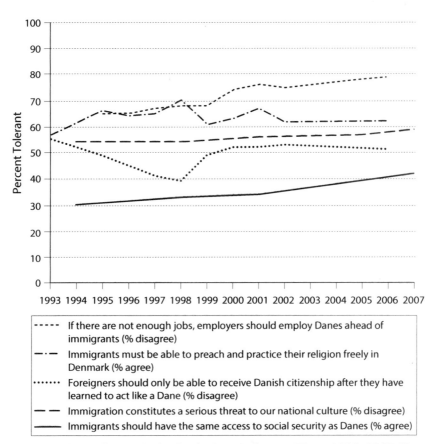

FIGURE 2.2 Immigrant Attitudes in Denmark over Time, 1993–2007 (Percent Tolerant Responses)

Note: The response categories were: completely agree; somewhat agree; somewhat disagree; completely disagree. For the data that does not appear in Togeby 2004, a "neither/nor" category was also included. To ensure comparability, this category has (along with "don't know" responses) been excluded from the percentage base. The population is restricted to eighteen- to seventy-year-olds. *Sources*: Data for the items about immigration as a cultural threat and immigrants' access to social security come from the Danish National Election Study (see Stubager, Holm, Smidstrup, and Kramb 2013). Data for the three remaining series comes from Togeby 2004 as well as our core survey (2006 observations).

that lies just beneath the surface to express itself publicly, we are at a loss to say what does.

Figure 2.2 displays responses to questions aimed at measuring hostility to immigrants in this series of studies. Consider first attitudes to discrimination in the labor market. The concern is: "If there are not

enough jobs, employers should employ Danes ahead of immigrants."
Rather than increasing over time as the threat of Islamic radicals became increasingly salient, or even spiking during the Cartoon Crisis,
opposition to a Danes-first policy steadily grows. A substantial majority always rejected this policy. Nonetheless, we see a steady increase
in the numbers opposing it, from two out of three to four out of five. If
intolerance toward immigrants was just below the surface, there was
an excess of events to legitimize an eruption of hostility toward immigrant minorities. In fact, the trend is toward a society progressively
more tolerant of them.

Stare at enough trend lines, and one is likely to come up with evidence for any idea one favors. It is therefore essential to determine
how representative this result is. As figure 2.2 shows, there has been a
steady trend in attitudes toward allowing immigrants access to social
security. Once again, it is in exactly the opposite direction that just
below the surface would predict. The proportion of the public agreeing
with this policy has increased, not decreased. All these changes, we
should emphasize, are modest in size. The dominant pattern in figure 2.2 is one of stability. Consider the perception of cultural threat.
The numbers rejecting the idea that "immigration constitutes a serious threat to our national character" are statistically interchangeable
over this whole period. So, too, with a few minor exceptions, are the
numbers rejecting the view that "foreigners should only be able to receive Danish citizenship after they have learned to act like a Dane."
And again with only minor qualification, so, too, are the numbers supporting the proposition that "immigrants must be able to preach and
practice their religion freely in Denmark." Nor, we want to underline,
can the absence of either a long-run trend or sharp spikes in hostility to
immigrants be explained by a lack of attention to events in the outside
world. Other research using the same data, thus, has shown that as the
situation in Kosovo worsened in 1999 and refugees started arriving in
Denmark, there was a marked increase in support of the view that "immigrants should have the same access to social security as Danes."[29]

Looking at the five trend lines in figure 2.2, we can find no proof
of resentment toward immigrants lurking in the shadows, waiting to

---

[29] See Togeby 2004, 62. Likewise, there was an increase in the support for "Denmark
receiving more refugees than we do today" in response to the event; see ibid., 58.

irrupt when a horrific event provides socially acceptable cover. Fifteen years is a considerable period of time. Tragically, it also is a period with no shortage of events that could serve as a pretext to express hostility toward Muslims. Yet the level of intolerance has not risen; indeed, in certain aspects, it has decreased. We cannot think of a way to reconcile the results in figure 2.2 with the just below the surface hypothesis.

There is a world of difference, however, between saying that there has been no upsurge in intolerance and that there is no problem of intolerance. For example, as figure 2.2 unmistakably demonstrates, there is no shortage of opposition to immigrants having freedom of religion—surely an integral civic right. Moreover, large numbers of Danes believe that immigrants should only be able to receive Danish citizenship when they have learned to behave like a Dane. To say that there has not been a surge in intolerance is not at all to say that there is a shortage of it.

THE PATTERN OF MEDIA COVERAGE AND POLITICAL PARTIES

A Surge in Media Attention

As we noted earlier, the publication of the cartoons depicting Moham-med ignited a political firestorm. The high drama of confrontations between Middle Eastern governments and the Danish government fea-tured emotional as well as literal incendiary protests (including mass demonstrations and the burning of a Danish embassy). Yet we have seen that Danes drew a clear distinction between Islamic fundamen-talists and Muslims. No less striking, they backed the civil rights of Muslims as fully as they did those of Danish groups—most remarkably, born-again Christians.

Political crises have a life history, though. The standard life his-tory of a crisis goes as follows. The crisis erupts without warning. It immediately gets massive media coverage. The public, for once fully attentive to politics, is alarmed. Then the public drama of the crisis typically plays itself out, usually within a relatively short period of time—sometimes months or even weeks.

Everyone can call to mind a crisis that fits this template. Yet just as individuals have their distinct life histories, so, too, do crises. Figure

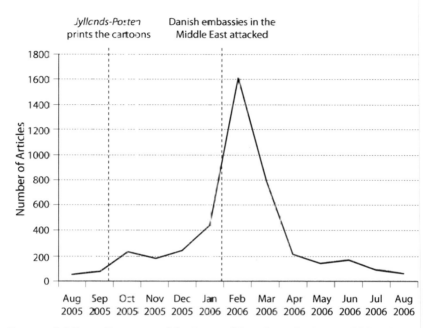

FIGURE 2.3 Press Coverage of the Issue of Free Speech, August 2005–August 2006 (Number of Articles)

Note: The figure displays the monthly number of articles in the Infomedia database from the newspapers *Jyllands-Posten* and *Politiken* as well as the Ritzaus Bureau newswires containing the word *ytringsfrihed* (freedom of speech). The three sources are chosen on the grounds that *Politiken* is a large newspaper to the left of the middle on the Danish political spectrum, *Jyllands-Posten* is to the right of the middle, and Ritzaus Bureau can be seen as representing all the smaller newspapers.

2.3 traces the media biography of the Cartoon Crisis, tracking the number of newspaper articles in the major newspapers dealing with the central issue—freedom of speech—from the Danish point of view.

A moment's glance at figure 2.3 makes it clear that the Cartoon Crisis went through three phases.[30] The issue of freedom of speech, in the form of a concern about self-censorship, had gradually become a subject of attention before the publication of the cartoons. With their publication, the level of media attention picked up, which is not a surprise. What should be a surprise is that it stayed at a relatively low level, on the order of two hundred articles per month, for nearly three months after the cartoons' publication.

[30] More formally, the shape of the distribution is distinctly leptokurtic.

This slow takeoff pattern is the opposite of the stereotypical image of a crisis erupting like a volcano. Why did what one might well expect to happen not happen? Because something else that one might stereotypically have expected to happen did not happen. Yes, a small number of imams gave inflammatory interviews. Sheikh Hlayhel, a local firebrand, declared that "democracy as practiced in Denmark is worth nothing to Muslims," and demanded an apology and retraction by the newspaper.[31] But all in all, the reaction of Muslims in Denmark was remarkably restrained: a demonstration in Copenhagen; a few press releases and emails; and a call for a sleep-in and strike that was ignored—in other words, a moderate reaction.

The self-restraint of Danish Muslims is all the more noteworthy in the face of what, from the point of view of many of them, was blasphemy; still more so viewed against the harsh rhetoric of the Danish People's Party. For example, a year before the issue of free speech topped the agenda, Mogens Camre, a member of the European Parliament for the Danish People's Party, asserted that "Islam does not belong in Europe, and our first priority must be to repatriate the Muslims. Islam is a threat to our future and we want to prevent Islam from setting any agenda in Europe. That faith belongs in a dark past and its political objective is just as destructive as that of Nazism. Islam must not be allowed the possibility to take Europe from us."[32]

Many, perhaps most, Danes take exception to the Danish People's Party. What is telling, however, is that the party's spokespeople feel free to be highly provocative. Coupling Islam and Nazism would likely end the career of a politician in the United States. Doing so in Denmark is a way of making a career. In a time and place where political leaders can publicly argue against the legitimacy of Islam as a religion, the restrained response of Muslims in Denmark during the Cartoon Crisis deserves all the more to be underlined.

Phase two of the crisis dramatically differed from phase one. As figure 2.3 shows, there is a stunning spike in media attention. Beginning in late November, the number of articles referring to freedom of speech

---

[31] Quoted in Klausen 2009, 87.
[32] Excerpt from Camre's speech at the Danish People's Party annual meeting in 2004. Quoted in Seidenfaden and Larsen 2006, 27.

leaps from approximately two hundred per month to sixteen hundred per month in February 2006.

What brought the issue of the cartoons to crisis levels of attention? Mid-November, several Pakistani imams offered bounties, which got wide circulation on the Internet, for the assassination of the cartoon illustrators. Twice in December, a delegation of imams from Denmark went to Beirut, Cairo, and Damascus, appealing for support. Weirdly, a word that does not quite capture what happened, they brought with them—in addition to the twelve original cartoons—other alleged depictions of the prophet Mohammed. One of the other pictures presented Mohammed as a pedophile rapist. Another depicted a French pig-squealing contestant accompanied by the caption, "Here is the real image of Muhammad."[33] They added these to their dossier as though they were cartoons that had been published in the Danish newspaper. Subsequently, partly in response to a reprinting of the cartoons in Sweden, a boycott of Danish products was launched in the Middle East. Three weeks later, the Danish embassies in Beirut and Damascus were attacked and the one in Beirut burned. Mass demonstrations in Middle Eastern countries were mounted several days later.

The sharp spike in the number of articles referring to freedom of speech in Danish newspapers was a response to Muslims outside, not inside, Demark who had launched protests and taken violent actions—with the acquiescence and sometimes at the prompting of governments in the Middle East, above all Egypt. In contrast, in Denmark, not only were Muslim immigrants not marching or demanding apologies, the association Democratic Muslims was established, specifically devoted to the mission of promoting reconciliation. But center stage from mid-January through late February was dominated by the boycott of Danish goods in the Middle East, the desecration of the Danish flag in the West Bank, and mass demonstrations of up to seven hundred thousand participants across the Muslim world.

Then, almost as suddenly as the crisis erupted, the political fever broke. From a high of sixteen hundred articles per month referring to freedom of speech, the number dropped to two hundred in April, and

---

[33] Every August, the French town of Trie Sur Baïse arranges the Festival of the Pig, part of which is a competition to imitate pig noises.

then fell off sharply over the next two months, virtually disappearing by August 2006. Phase three, the disappearance of the issue of freedom of speech from the public agenda, was thus the mirror image of phase one, the appearance of the issue on the public agenda. A metaphoric summary of the salience of the crisis—expressed in terms of the absolute number of articles published on free speech—is an initially low-grade fever erupting suddenly, spiking relatively briefly, and then breaking and falling off.

Partisan Elite Framing

In crises, ordinary citizens take their lead from political elites. If the parties react with competing interpretations of what is happening and what should be done about it, citizens will tend to stand with the party they identify with. On the other hand, if the parties present a united front disregarding partisan considerations, the public will tend to follow their lead by also disregarding partisan considerations.[34]

How, then, did the leaders of the political parties react to the crisis? To provide a systematic picture, we conducted a separate content analysis of the two leading national newspapers, one leaning to the right, and the other to the left, focusing on articles covering the reactions of the politically influential to the crisis.[35] Specifically, for each party leader, we identified articles in the relevant time period where the party leader was directly quoted with a statement on the crisis. Next, we coded each of these articles for the presence of one or more specified frames (e.g., a free speech or tolerance frame). The unit of analysis is thus each statement by a party leader.[36] This procedure supplies a precise mapping of how each party attempted to frame the Cartoon Crisis.

Panel A of figure 2.4 shows a politically focused analysis of the reactions of the leaders of the political parties. The issue did erupt rapidly,

[34] The discovery of the two forms that partisan top-down influence takes and their impact on public opinion was made by Richard Brody (1991). For its seminal exposition, see Zaller 1992.

[35] The right-of-center newspaper was *Jyllands-Posten*, which published the cartoons; the left-of-center paper was *Politiken*.

[36] This means that some articles were coded in relation to two or more party leaders (and as such, are counted two or more times in the content analysis). For details of this analysis, see the online appendix (http://press.princeton.edu/titles/10400.html).

rising from fifty articles (quoting a party leader) in January to two hundred in early February. In terms of elite politics, however, rather than spiking briefly, the issue stayed on the front pages for a period of months. Then, consistent with the national interest, the attention of party leaders to the issue dropped rapidly.

The crux of the matter, though, is not how often party leaders spoke about the issue but instead what they said about it. Broadly, two themes were available to them. The crisis could be framed in terms of a defense of the principle of freedom of speech. Alternatively (but not mutually exclusively), it could be framed in terms of the importance of tolerance. The politics of the crisis obviously differ depending on how the issue is framed. Panel B of figure 2.4 accordingly tracks the salience of the two frames over the life history of the crisis.

The free speech frame always was the dominant theme. The only qualification is that the two become trivially comparable in frequency of appearance at the end of the crisis—trivially comparable, we say, because of the infrequency of the appearance of both. Even so, it is worth noting that the tolerance frame increased at roughly the same rate as the free speech frame as the crisis approached its high point. We read this as an indication that Danish party leaders saw the dangers of a backlash against Muslims from the start of the crisis and stepped up their efforts to thwart it as the crisis heightened. As the crisis played itself out, the free speech frame again dominated the tolerance frame.

What politicians were talking about is important, but which ones were talking about what is even more so. Figure 2.5 displays, in the form of bars, the proportion of times that the leaders of the political parties framed their remarks in terms of free speech or tolerance.

Some differences in the reactions of the political parties can be detected, provided one examines figure 2.5 with microscopic attention. Looking to the left in the figure as well as the political landscape, the Red-Green Alliance placed the most emphasis on the value of tolerance. In fact, it was the only party to talk more about tolerance than free speech during the crisis. For all other parties, the balance of the rhetoric went the other way.

This qualification noted, the dominant feature of figure 2.5 is consensus. With the exception of the smallest party in the parliament, the

A

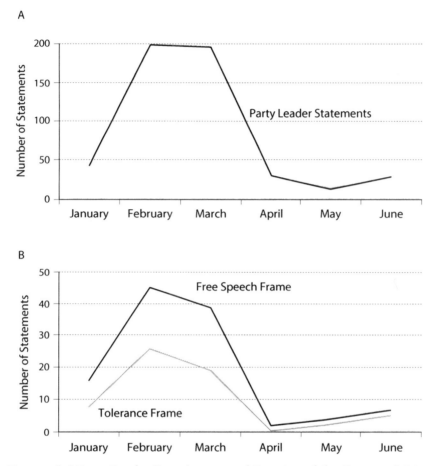

FIGURE 2.4 Party Leader Reactions to and Framing of the Cartoon Crisis, January–June 2006 (Number of Statements)

Note: Panel A shows the number of articles in the newspapers *Politiken* and *Jyllands-Posten* where party leaders were directly quoted with a statement on the cartoon crisis. Panel B shows the number of statements where the "free speech frame" and "tolerance frame," respectively, were present. For procedure, coding, and details, see the online appendix.

freedom of speech frame dominated the tolerance frame for parties ranging from the left through to the party farthest to the right (the Danish People's Party). In other words, when Danes looked to their political leaders for guidance about what was at stake in the crisis, the answer they got was freedom of speech.

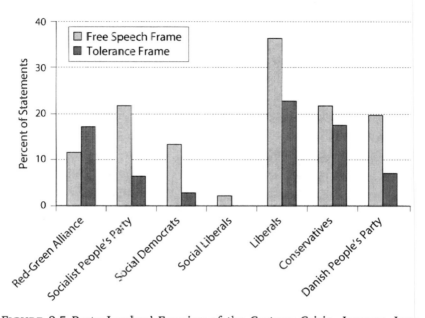

FIGURE 2.5 Party Leaders' Framing of the Cartoon Crisis, January–June 2006 (Percent of Statements)

Note: The figure shows the percentage of each party leader's statements that contained each of the two frames. For procedure, coding, and details, see figure 2.4 and the online appendix.

TOP-DOWN POLITICS AND THE SUBSIDING OF A RALLY IN DEFENSE OF DEMOCRATIC VALUES

How did Danes respond to the challenge of the Cartoon Crisis? They defended democratic rights, including those of Muslims. But is this a story about citizens, or alternatively, opinion leaders?

Our stream of data on popular support for political rights began at the height of the crisis and continued through its disappearance from the public agenda. We have no comparable measures before the crisis, and given this, cannot see how citizens reacted as the mass media and politicians concentrated their attention on the crisis.[37] And we have seen that throughout this period, there was a barrage of messages in support of liberal democratic values. Two values in particular were the

[37] Cf. figure 2.4.

focus. One was freedom of speech, invoked in defense of the right of newspapers to publish on controversial subjects. The other was tolerance, invoked in defense of the right of immigrants in Denmark to be accepted as part of the larger society.

Not surprisingly, the public debate was one-sided. We coded the valence or direction of each statement framed in terms of free speech or tolerance. In almost all cases, the presence of a given frame means unconditional support for free speech or tolerance, respectively. The only instances of qualified support for free speech are two statements by the Red-Green Alliance, and the only cases of conditional support for tolerance are three statements from the Danish People's Party.

Most studies of political rallies of public opinion concentrate on the surge phase—the initial shift of public opinion in response to elite influence—in order to demonstrate the influence of top-down politics. Lacking measures of public opinion before the crisis, we will look at the subsiding phase—the subsequent shift of public opinion as elites and the media turn their attention to other issues on the agenda. To catch a glimpse of public opinion as the crisis receded, we have divided the data into two time periods, when the media concentration on freedom of speech and tolerance was at its height, and when the issue had effectively, for all intents and purposes, fallen off the public agenda. The first comprises respondents interviewed in March and April; the second those interviewed between May and July.

Two measurement limitations deserve emphatic emphasis. The first is temporal. The time period our study covers is more limited than it appears: the bulk of the interviews were done over the three-month stretch from the beginning of March through the end of May.[38] The second is methodological. The respondents interviewed toward the end of a survey tend to be those who have been most difficult to contact or persuade. They may, and frequently do, differ from the more cooperative respondents in a number of respects, some of which may bear on

[38] Support for civil rights was measured only in the second survey (running from March 2 to August 20, 2006), and the bulk of the interviews in this round were done from March 2 through May 31 (n = 1,798; 91.4 percent). The last group of interviews (n = 169) was conducted in June through August as the polling company had to draw a new sample of individuals from the Central Person Registry because the response rate turned out to be a bit lower than expected.

TABLE 2.4 Political Tolerance by Time of Interview, Average for
All Groups (Percent)

	March–April	May–July	Difference (p-value in parentheses)
Debate	74	62	−11
			(< 0.001)
Demonstrate	73	73	0
			(0.909)
Speak at high schools	60	54	−6
			(0.029)
Oppose telephone tapping	40	40	0
			(0.816)

Note: N varies from 1,774 to 1,794. Entries are percentage tolerant responses after controlling for gender, age (categorized into 18–29, 30–39, 40–49, 50–59, and 60–70), county of residence (based on the fifteen pre-2007 counties), education (categorized into only primary, vocational upper secondary [i.e., craftsman], short-cycle tertiary [further vocational training], medium-cycle tertiary [e.g., schoolteacher or nurse], and long-cycle tertiary [MA level and beyond]), political knowledge (low, medium, or high), and political interest (very, somewhat, only slightly, or not at all interested). For the wording of the rights question, see table 2.2.

any differences observed between them.[39] Accordingly, in estimating levels of support for civil rights, we have controlled for gender, age, county of residence, education, political knowledge, and political interest. The risk of invalid inference cannot be eliminated, but this rare opportunity to catch sight of a rally of the public as it subsides persuades us that the risk is worth taking.

Table 2.4 depicts the mean levels of support for the quartet of rights we tracked in the two periods. Support levels for three of the four values during these two times are essentially the same.[40] For example,

[39] Appendix C contains a close comparison of the two subsamples. The analyses reveal that the polling agency concentrated its efforts in different geographic parts of the country during the two periods. This has advantages as well as disadvantages. On the positive side, it means that the two subsamples differ less in terms of their composition of easy- and hard-to-reach respondents simply because most respondents in the second subsample were not contacted in March–April. On the negative side, it also means that there is a large geographic difference between the two subsamples. There are also some minor differences in terms of age, education, and political interest. Hence the controls mentioned in the text.

[40] There is an arguable exception. In March and April, 60 percent supported the rights of groups to speak at high schools; in May through July, the number was 54 percent. We do not want to make too much of this, partly because the right to speak at schools

support for the right to demonstrate stayed at precisely the same level. In March and April, it was 73 percent; in May through July, it was again 73 percent. The one exception to the pattern of stability is the right to take part in public debate. In March and April, the level of support for freedom of speech, averaged across the eight groups, was 74 percent. In May–July, it was 62 percent. We observe, in short, change between the two periods in the positions of the public on only one political right—that is, freedom of speech.

Table 2.4 summarizes support for civil rights averaged across the eight groups. A question therefore springs to mind: Is the change in support for free speech driven by large changes for only a few groups, or does the shift in media attention affect Danes' views on the rights of all (or nearly all) our groups? The answer can be found in table 2.5, which breaks down the first row of table 2.4 group by group. With one exception, the pattern is clear. For seven of the eight groups there was a drop in support by at least 10 percentage points for the group's freedom of speech. The only exception is the group with the lowest level of support from the start: neo-Nazis. For this group we record a small increase in support for its freedom of speech from the height to the aftermath of the crisis. The change is neither substantively nor statistically significant, however. These findings suggest that the strong focus on the right of freedom of speech found in elite discourse during the crisis boosted public support for this core democratic right across the range of contentious groups in society, although again we want to underscore our lack of evidence of levels of support for freedom of speech before the crisis.

The specificity of the public's reaction, with a change evident only with respect to the value immediately bound up in the crisis, speaks to the terms in which the interactions between voters and elites should be understood. Traditionally, there was a bottom-up emphasis in the study of elections: candidates and parties responded to the preferences of voters. Recently, more attention has been given to top-down models.[41] The

---

has, as mentioned earlier, at best a highly derivative claim to be a right, and particularly because the drop in support is not obviously politically significant.

[41] The term *top-down model*, it should be remarked, is systematically ambiguous. It sometimes has a deliberately narrow meaning, referring specifically to the role of partisan elites in defining the menu of alternatives on offer to citizens. For theoretical discussions of this, see Sniderman 2000; Sniderman and Bullock 2004. For an empirical test, see Petersen, Slothuus, and Togeby 2010. Still more often, the term is used as part

TABLE 2.5 Change in Support for Free Speech of Groups from the Height of the Crisis to Its Disappearance from the Public Agenda (Percent)

	March–April	May–July	Difference (p-value in parentheses)
Muslims	77	62	−15 (0.002)
Born-again Christians	80	68	−11 (0.026)
Far Left	86	74	−12 (0.009)
Far Right	82	72	−10 (0.027)
Islamic fundamentalists	62	48	−14 (0.007)
Autonome	81	71	−10 (0.037)
Bikers	64	50	−15 (0.006)
Neo-Nazis	54	57	+4 (0.509)

Note: N varies from 433 to 486. Entries are percentage tolerant responses after controlling for gender, age, county of residence, education, political knowledge, and political interest (cf. table 2.4). For the wording of the rights question, see table 2.2.

premise of such models is that the supporters of candidates and parties are dutifully responsive to the persuasive communications of political elites.[42] Like most formulations, it can be offered in an extreme or moderate version. In the more extreme version, it is as though political elites are puppet masters pulling the strings of puppet voters. In the more moderate version, it is more a matter of voters picking up the positions of candidates that they themselves already were predisposed to hold.

Our findings are both consistent with and point to the limits of moderate versions of top-down models. The pressure to support the principle of freedom of speech was intense, as we have seen. And inasmuch

of an elite definition of the alternatives on offer, and implies a claim that voters take the positions they do in response to the cues or persuasive communications of political elites. For the seminal work in this regard, see Zaller 1992.

[42] Bullock 2011; Druckman, Peterson, and Slothuus 2013; Lenz 2009; Slothuus 2010; Slothuus and de Vreese 2010.

as our study can speak to the responsiveness of mass publics to elite communications, it supports the hypothesis of top-down influence. Contrary to what could have been expected, the majority of Danes did not show signs of a backlash against Muslims. If anything, they increased their support for the right of Muslims to take part in public debate. At the same time, we only saw an increase in support for the particular value that was the focal point of elite communications. One might have supposed that the closest kindred of the value of freedom of speech—namely, freedom of assembly—might have picked up some support, too, and yet it did not. This suggests that top-down influence tends to be specific, not diffuse. It also indicates that the effects of elite communications tend to be short-lived, persisting only as long as the communications continue.[43] Levels of political tolerance soon returned to the—lower—equilibrium we suspect that we would have discovered in the months leading up to the crisis.[44]

We want to stress that top-down influence is not a synonym for the elite manipulation of citizens' views. The framing of the crisis dominant in elite discourse resonated with many citizens' preexisting views of also valuing free speech for minority groups, even before the crisis (cf. table 2.5).[45] Yet the role of elite communications is an important part of our story about the Cartoon Crisis. We can only speculate what would have happened to levels of tolerance—specifically, to the reaction toward Muslims in Denmark—if elites had chosen to frame the crisis as an irresolvable conflict between cultures. Playing on prejudice against outgroups as a political strategy has worked before, and it will work again.

An Alternative Interpretation: The Logic of Reciprocity

The question that we have asked is whether there was a backlash against the minority. It is the key query because its answer speaks to the democratic character of Danish society. There was every reason

---

[43] Chong and Druckman 2010.

[44] Analyses of aggregate public opinion over time by Benjamin Page and Robert Shapiro (1992) and Togeby (2004) are consistent with this interpretation.

[45] In this sense, the Cartoon Crisis is parallel to what as an experiment could be labeled a "facilitative design," where participants are exposed to "a directional force in the form of a relevant reason to do what people are already predisposed to do" (Sniderman 2011, 108).

to believe that the assaultive reactions of Islamic radicals and Muslim governments to the publication of the cartoons would ignite a firestorm of reaction against Muslims in Denmark—a demonization of Muslims along with a denial of their civil rights. In actuality, the majority drew a sharp distinction between Islamic fundamentalists and Muslims, and gave as much support to the civil rights of Muslims as to other admittedly contentious but undeniably legitimate groups in Danish society.

We believe that the fact Danes kept their democratic balance in a political storm speaks to the capacity of ordinary citizens to discharge the duties of democratic citizenship. But our findings can be given an interpretation quite different from ours. It was the majority's rights— above all, their right to freedom of speech—that was being challenged. Is it not possible that their support for the rights of the Muslim minority was the price of their supporting their own rights? How could they justify their having a right to freedom of expression without acknowledging that the Muslim minority had this right, too? We call this the reciprocity hypothesis.

The premise here is that Danes supported the rights of Muslims in order to cement their claim to the same rights. On its face, there is something curious about this reasoning. Consider the well-documented reactions of US citizens to rights of Communists and other suspect groups during the McCarthy era. They did not at all presume that to be secure in their own civil rights, they must swarm to the defense of the rights of Communists, atheists, and the like; quite to the contrary. All the evidence backs the view that to the extent US citizens made a connection between the two, it was that subversive groups were all the more dangerous if they had the same rights as loyal citizens. Indeed, that was precisely the point of denying that they had a right to freedom of expression and assembly: if these subversive groups were free to propagate their ideas, they would be all the more of a threat. There is a different way to put the same stance. If there is one proposition securely established by research on political tolerance, it is this: the more threatening a group is perceived to be, the less support there will be for its enjoying political rights.[46] On either line of reasoning, Danes

---

[46] John Sullivan, James Piereson, and George Marcus (1982) are responsible for generating this hypothesis as well as assembling a compelling body of evidence in support of it. James Gibson has also made seminal contributions; see, for example, Gibson 2006; Gibson and Gouws 2003.

should give less support to the rights of Muslims than to those of fellow Danes under the strain of a real crisis. But we know that just the opposite happened: they give as much support to the rights of Muslims as to those of fellow Danes.

We can bring more evidence to bear. If the reactions of Danes fit the usual pattern of clashes over civil rights, Danes should be more likely to perceive—and be willing to say that they perceived—Muslims as a threat when the crisis was at its most tense than when it was over. On the other hand, if our narrative is right, the reactions of Danes should not fit the standard pattern precisely because they perceived Muslims not to be transgressive and therefore not to be a threat. And to put our reasoning to a still-tougher test, Danes should be no more (or not much more) likely to perceive Muslims to be a threat when the clash was at its most intense than when it had faded from public attention.

Table 2.6 accordingly presents how threatening Muslims (and other groups) were perceived to be to Danish society in the earlier part of our study, March and April, when the crisis was at the forefront of attention, and the latter part of our study, May through July, when it was yesterday's news. Consistent with our argument, far from responding with alarm to Muslims when the crisis erupted, Danes viewed Muslims as among the least threatening groups (M = 0.45) both when the clash was most intense and when the tension had largely dissipated (M = 0.45)

Yet one more line of evidence is relevant. Almost by design, one can say that a person who feels threatened will favor measures to control or preferably eliminate the threat. One way to do so is for the police to keep a closer eye on the threatening group—for example, in the form of increased tapping of their telephones. It follows that if the standard version of top-down influence is the whole story of the Cartoon Crisis, there should be less opposition to police tapping the phones of Muslims during the crisis than when the issue has receded from public attention. In table 2.7 we submit this implication to a test.

Focus on Muslims in this table. The numbers record the level of opposition to wiretapping. In March–April, 58 percent opposed wiretapping Muslims; by May–July, only 46 percent opposed it. In a word, support for the civil rights was higher when the crisis was at its height than when it abated. Now examine the responses to the other groups. The levels of opposition to wiretappng born-again Christians, the Autonome, and bikers either didn't change between March–April and

TABLE 2.6 Change in Perception of Threat from Groups from the Height of the Crisis to Its Disappearance from the Public Agenda (Scale Scores)

	March–April	May–July	Difference (p-value in parentheses)
Muslims	0.45	0.45	0
			(0.885)
Born-again Christians	0.45	0.42	− 3
			(0.037)
Far Left	0.42	0.38	− 4
			(0.003)
Far Right	0.54	0.47	− 6
			($<$ 0.001)
Islamic fundamentalists	0.78	0.78	0
			(0.835)
Autonome	0.50	0.49	− 1
			(0.527)
Bikers	0.55	0.55	0
			(0.828)
Neo-Nazis	0.65	0.65	0
			(0.749)

Note: N varies from 1,765 to 1,864. Entries are mean scores on a 0–1 scale after controlling for gender, age, county of residence, education, political knowledge, and political interest (cf. table 2.4). Question wording: "I will now list a number of groups in Denmark and ask how great a threat you believe each of them pose to Danish society. Please respond on a scale from 0 to 10, 0 indicating that the group is not threatening at all, 10 indicating that the group is very threatening." Answers were rescaled to run from 0 to 1.

May–July or they increased. Muslims are the only group that enjoyed more support for its right to privacy when the crisis was at its peak than when it had faded away.

What does the evidence boil down to? Danes gave the same level of support for the civil rights of Muslims as they did to fellow Danes, and one reason they were able to do so is because they did not perceive Muslims as a threat. But does this mean that the finding that we have attached so much importance to—that there was a solid wall of support for the rights of Muslims—really was only to be expected?[47] Not at all. The whole point is that notwithstanding the crisis atmosphere,

[47] There is a crucial sense in which our findings were to be expected. Contrary to an impression of our findings being at odds with previous research, they are consistent with it. Conditional on knowing that Muslims were not perceived as a threat, and setting aside the quite reasonable expectation of prejudice toward them as well as spillover of hostility toward Islamic radicals, the prediction should be support for the rights of Muslims.

TABLE 2.7 Change in Opposition to Telephone Tapping of Groups from the Height of the Crisis to Its Disappearance from the Public Agenda (Percent)

	March–April	May–July	Difference (p-value in parentheses)
Muslims	58	46	−11 (0.032)
Born-again Christians	53	55	+2 (0.690)
Far Left	62	48	−14 (0.014)
Far Right	37	42	+5 (0.347)
Islamic fundamentalists	16	23	+7 (0.052)
Autonome	40	42	+2 (0.706)
Bikers	27	30	+2 (0.620)
Neo-Nazis	19	31	+11 (0.016)

Note: N varies from 436 to 482. Entries are percentage tolerant responses after controlling for gender, age, county of residence, education, political knowledge, and political interest (cf. table 2.4). For the wording of the rights question, see table 2.2.

real threats made and carried out during the crisis, striking levels of fear of Islamic fundamentalists, and widespread fear and resentment of as well as hostility toward immigrants before the crisis, ordinary citizens' perception of Muslims nonetheless remained reality based.[48] And they were not perceived as a threat.

A LAST WORD

When it counted most, when the clash was most intense and the outcome most uncertain, a decisive majority of ordinary citizens stood

[48] Regarding Islamic fundamentalists, we find that on the perceived threat scale, which runs from 0 to 1, the mean score for Islamic fundamentalists is 0.8, the median is 0.9, and the mode is 1. Regarding the relationship between attitudes toward immigrants and Muslims, the term *immigrants* is not an exact synonym for *Muslim*. Yet it is largely so. In a confirmatory factor analysis, we have found a clearly unacceptable fit for a model forcing attitudes to immigrants and Muslims to load on the same dimension. A model with separate factors for immigrant and Muslim attitudes yields a clearly superior fit, albeit the two factors correlate at 0.85.

behind the civil rights of Muslims; in fact, they gave them fully as much support as they did fellow Danes like born-again Christians. We know of no one, particularly including ourselves, who predicted this response to the crisis. Indeed, we are not aware of anyone, now excluding ourselves, who subsequently has realized that. It is a striking example of ordinary citizens coming up to the mark. It is deeply instructive that Danes treat Muslims the same as they treat Danish groups like born-again Christians. And it is still more illustrative that they do so even though so many of them dislike, resent, and disdain immigrants. But in truth, this is only the beginning of an argument on behalf of the democratic faith.

In T. S. Eliot's play *Murder in the Cathedral*, Thomas Becket, once chancellor of England and closest friend of Henry V, the king of England, but now archbishop of Canterbury and accordingly at odds with his king, seeks sanctuary in a church. Banging on the church door and demanding admission are four knights from Henry's court. They have come to kill Becket because they believe Henry wishes his death. Before deciding to open the door, Becket is presented with four temptations, the last being that in opening the door, he may be willing his own martyrdom, and he responds:

The last temptation is the greatest treason:
To do the right deed for the wrong reason.

So it is here. In supporting Muslims' claims to civil rights every bit as fully as they support the rights of other controversial though legitimate groups, even at the height of a crisis over the legitimate place of Islamic values in the Danish culture, Danish citizens "[did] the right deed." But it can still be asked, Did they do it for the right reason?[49]

---

[49] For an answer to this question, see chapter 5.

CHAPTER 3

The Covenant Paradox

From the eighteenth century on, European commentators and intellectuals have flagged racism as a signal of US failing, a blood-red thread running through the US experience from the past to the present. They have similarly noted the absence of a social safety net as a signal of US failing, as evidence that the US state is a halfway station, affirming the political principles of a democratic politics but evading its social obligations.

The censure of European public intellectuals can be justified. Their complacency cannot. Anyone who can draw breath can see that western Europe, too, is struggling with the inclusion of immigrants, and above all, Muslim immigrants. In particular, many fear that the welfare state now faces an existential dilemma. On the one side, the provision of a universal safety net is the moral principle that separates the United States as a halfway station from a welfare state like Denmark. The benefits of the welfare state, on the other side, are a magnet attracting immigrant minorities, but the costs of providing these benefits to immigrant minorities are in the largest measure borne by native citizens. The result, the argument runs, is a negative dialectic. The welfare state won and held the loyalty of voters, so long as "people believed they were paying the social welfare part of their taxes to people who were like themselves."[1] As increasing numbers of immigrants become the beneficiaries, increasing numbers of citizens ask themselves, why should "we" make sacrifices so that "they" benefit? The outcome: popular support for the welfare state is leaking away.

[1] Wolfe and Klausen 1997.

Two concerns are coupled here: anxiety about a loss of support for the welfare state, and apprehension that the loss is due to fears, resentments, and stereotypes directed against immigrants. Support for the welfare state in Denmark is high and indeed consensual across the whole of the political spectrum, as we will show. Yet there is no questioning the sincerity, if that is quite the right word, of the anger and resentment of many Danes toward immigrants. The first concern is not justified, as we will demonstrate, but the second is, although not in the way that has been supposed. The moral covenant underpinning the welfare state simultaneously promotes equal treatment for (some) immigrants and provides a platform for discrimination against (other) immigrants. This is a second paradox of liberal democracy—the covenant paradox.

The objective of this chapter is to present a theory of the covenant paradox. The job we are asking this theory to do is not a modest one. Its first responsibility is to specify under what conditions and why the moral premises of the welfare state favor the equal treatment of immigrants. Its second responsibility is to specify under what conditions and why the very same moral premises open the door to discrimination against immigrants. The key to these contradictory outcomes, we will show, is the temporal logic of evaluative judgments. Prospective judgments of benefits and obligations favor equal treatment. Retrospective judgments, again of benefits and obligations, pave the way for discriminatory treatment.

IMMIGRATION AND SUPPORT FOR THE WELFARE STATE

The concern that increasing numbers of non-Western immigrants will undermine public support for the welfare state in western Europe has been fueled by research from the United States. Alberto Alesina and Edward Glaeser's (2004) finding of a negative relationship between ethnic heterogeneity and spending on welfare across US cities and states figures prominently in this debate. Likewise, survey data reveal that white Americans' negative attitudes toward blacks correlate strongly with opposition to welfare spending.[2] Perhaps the most direct evidence of a similar dynamic in western Europe comes from a recent study of

---

[2] Gilens 1999.

Sweden—a country that is the prototypical example of the universal welfare state, known for its egalitarian society, and with no recent history of pervasive ethnic diversity.[3] In Sweden, the number of immigrants at the county level does turn out to have significant negative effects on support for the welfare state. Moreover, *changes* in the number of immigrants (i.e., recent immigration) in a county have a negative effect on attitudes toward universal spending. These findings together prove "clear evidence that ethnic heterogeneity negatively affects support for social welfare expenditure—even in Sweden."[4]

The evidence is not one-sided, though. In arguably the most comprehensive empirical analysis at the level of policy, Richard Johnson, Keith Banting, Will Kymlicka, and Stuart Soroka (2010) conclude (with appropriate cautions) that there is no compelling proof of a connection between the adoption of multicultural policies and an erosion of the welfare state.[5] Still, European scholars have found structures in welfare attitudes that mirror the US experiences. One example is Christian Albrekt Larsen's (2011) study of the US public's perceptions and attitudes compared, as systematically as the available data allow, to similar perceptions and attitudes among the publics in Britain, Sweden, and Denmark. There is a remarkable similarity of results across the four countries: Europeans have at least as negative stereotypes about outgroups (that is, non-Western immigrants) as Americans have against blacks, and there are consistent, nontrivial correlations between negative stereotypes and the lack of support for welfare spending directed toward immigrants, the poor, and even redistribution more generally. Based on these findings, Larsen (ibid., 351) concludes, "It is not a matter of whether the American pattern will come to be replicated in Europe. The data clearly indicate that it has already happened."[6] His observation fits hand in glove with Martin Gilens's (1999) classic

---

[3] *Universalist* is preferred by some as a more precise term for the welfare state regime we call universal. For a state-of-the-art status of the universal or "Nordic" welfare state model, see Kvist et al. 2012. For the seminal reference, see Esping-Andersen 1990.

[4] Eger 2010, 203.

[5] See also Kymlicka and Banting 2006.

[6] Another study, using data from the European Social Survey, similarly finds that "negative attitudes towards immigrants are strongly associated with less support for the welfare state, independently of the perceived presence of immigrants" (Senik, Stichnoth, and Van der Straeten 2009, 361). It also shows that the average effect across countries masks important differences between countries and regions.

study of race and welfare in the United States. A large number of white Americans are strongly opposed to welfare because they believe black Americans are taking advantage of it. Evidently, it is not necessary to have a generous welfare state to evoke a "they're lazy and ripping off the system" response; an ungenerous welfare policy does the trick, too.

When results of first-class research clash, a prudent strategy is to step back from what is clearly a complex dispute and find a simple starting point. What do studies directly measuring attitudes toward the welfare state show? The same data demonstrating a negative relationship between immigration and welfare support at the county level in Sweden also reveal an aggregate increase in welfare support over the years.[7] In fact, most systematic data tracking public opinion over time and across countries find remarkably stable—and high—levels of public support for welfare state policies in western Europe. Not every country is like every other, and not every social welfare regime is like every other social welfare regime.[8] But the general trend is high and stable support, and in some countries in western Europe public support for welfare services has even increased in recent years.[9]

We do not at all wish to gainsay the grinding resentment at immigrations "exploitation" of the welfare state. But purely at a descriptive level, it does not appear that non-Western immigration has undercut citizens' willingness to support a generous welfare state. Other forces seem to be at work in favor of maintaining high levels of support for government-provided welfare. One possible explanation might be higher levels of employment and economic growth in the period following the 1970s and 1980s, leading to less economic hardship and making a large

[7] Eger 2010; see Maureen Eger's figure 2 along with the positive coefficients for "year" in tables 2 and 3.

[8] For analyses and discussion of differences in welfare support across welfare state regimes as well as the major individual-level explanations, see Andress and Heien 2001; Blekesaune and Quadagno 2003; Gelissen 2000; Jæger 2009; Larsen 2006; Svallfors 1997. See also Eger 2010, specifically figure 2 along with the positive coefficients for "year" in tables 2 and 3, which show an aggregate increase in welfare support over the years in Sweden, too.

[9] For example, Clem Brooks and Jeff Manza (2007, 110–13) investigated trends in welfare attitudes during 1975–2000 in the United States, Sweden, Norway, and the Netherlands, and found little indication that public support for welfare is declining. Likewise, Jonas Edlund's (2009) study showed modest changes in welfare attitudes in twenty-two countries over a two-decade period. For further evidence, see Svallfors 2012. Mads Meier Jæger (2012) reports some deviations from this trend.

welfare state more financially sustainable.[10] Another explanation can be found in party politics. The popularity of the welfare state among voters shapes the competition for political power among partisan elites: when voters tend to prefer a generous welfare state, center-right parties move in the direction of supporting the welfare state in order to build a broad enough coalition among voters to win office.[11] With the issue of welfare cuts low on the partisan agenda, the public support for the welfare state is not politically challenged and a self-reinforcing dynamic is created, keeping public support for the welfare state high.

It may seem odd that this is so in light of the success of conservative parties in a number of western European countries, most especially Denmark. But politics is a more than equal opportunity enterprise. The major center-right party in Denmark, the Liberal Party, serves as a vivid illustration. In the years leading up to the election in 2001, the Liberal Party abandoned its earlier critical approach toward the welfare state, and instead proposed several popular welfare expansions on areas such as health care and help to families with children. Above all, the party committed to preserving and in some areas expanding the welfare state by making it more efficient. It was a piquant strategy: the political Right won its way to power as the savior of the welfare state.[12]

Not only do center-right parties, as in this example, need to conform to the pro-welfare attitudes of the electorate to gain power in countries where the parties on the left traditionally are strong; they might even "overcompensate" once in office by delivering larger increases in welfare spending than their center-left counterparts in order to persuade voters that they really are in favor of a welfare state. Discovering this phenomenon, Carsten Jensen (2010, 295) explains that "in left-wing-dominated countries, right-wing governments display the same basic spending behavior as left-wing governments—namely expansion. Needless to say, this is likely to produce continuing expansion of the welfare state as all governments, regardless of party color, rally behind the existing arrangements." It is precisely such strategic efforts by center-right parties, in rhetoric and action, to promote welfare state

[10] See discussion in Pierson 2001.

[11] For the seminal work, see Pierson 1994.

[12] Which is not to say that this strategy is a guarantee of perpetual power. As we write, the Left is in power in Denmark.

policies that is a likely candidate to explain the sustained high levels of support for the welfare state, as voters tend to follow cues from partisan elites when forming policy preferences.[13]

Welfare State Support in Denmark

All these lines of argument are general, possibly applicable in some places but not others, and at some times but not others. Hence, we begin our analysis by looking at support for the welfare state. To assess the level of support for the welfare state in Denmark, we asked the respondents to rate on a scale of 0 through 10 the importance of government financing for an array of welfare services. To ease comparison of our results with other studies, we examined a question often used in cross-national studies.[14] The policies break down into the two categories presented below in tables 3.1 and 3.2, respectively.

In table 3.1, the first four policies are examples of core welfare state commitments to the needy: the health care sector, home care for the elderly, disability pensions for people who are physically worn out, and education maintenance grants for students. The first column in the table makes it clear that there is overwhelming support for these policies—indeed, virtually universal support in the public taken as a whole.[15] The median importance score, out of a possible 10, is 10 for the government financing of health and home care for the elderly, 9 for support for disability pensions, and 8 for education maintenance grants, rehabilitation of drug addicts, retraining for the unemployed, and housing benefits for low-income households. As significant, popular support, policy by policy, is high across the ideological spectrum. As columns two through five show, there is no cleavage whatsoever between parties of the left and those of the right—including the radical Right—in support of the welfare state's core policies.

---

[13] Bullock 2011; Druckman, Peterson, and Slothuus 2013; Slothuus 2010; Slothuus and de Vreese 2010.

[14] We followed the question used by the International Social Survey Program. See Edlund 2009.

[15] In this and the following tables in this chapter, "all" or "overall mean" includes all our respondents regardless of their party preference (that is, including those who do not indicate a party affiliation, and hence are not counted in the partisan columns or rows).

TABLE 3.1 Importance of Welfare Services on Political Consensus Policies by Party

How important is government financing to the following?	All		Left wing		Social Liberals		Social Democrats		Center-Right		Danish People's Party	
	Median	Mode	Median	Mode	Median	Mode	Median	Mode	Median	Mode	Median	Mode
Health care sector	10	10	10	10	10	10	10	10	10	10	10	10
Home care for the elderly	10	10	10	10	9	10	10	10	9	10	10	10
Disability pensions for persons who are physically worn out	9	10	10	10	9	10	10	10	9	10	10	10
Education maintenance grants for students	8	10	10	10	8	10	9	10	8	8	8	10
Rehabilitation of drug addicts	8	10	9	10	8	10	8	10	8	8	8	10
Retraining for unemployed persons	8	10	8	10	8	8	8	10	7	8	8	10
Housing benefits for low-income households	8	10	8	10	8	8	8	10	7	8	8	10

Note: Support is measured on a scale from 0 through 10. Higher values indicate greater support. Question wording: "I would now like to hear what you think about whether the government should be financing the following areas. Please use a scale from 0 to 10, where 0 indicates that it is not an area that the government should attend to, and 10 indicates that it is an area that is very important for the government to attend to. Should the government finance . . . ?"

To say that citizens support the welfare state is not to claim that they support with equal fervor every social policy that governments may propose, and still less, that they cannot distinguish between the goals of the welfare state and the policy means to achieve them. In fact, the argument over how best to maintain the welfare state has been the rationale dominating Danish politics. Hence the irony of the center-right parties making a bid for political power on the grounds that they are the defenders of the welfare state. That the Center-Right chose this strategy testifies to the strong political consensus over the welfare state that is so evidently illustrated in table 3.1.

For all practical purposes, as table 3.1 makes plain, the first three policies command support across the ideological spectrum. They are policies that have no politics. The next four also are at the center of the covenant to help the needy, but arithmetically, the mean level of support for these policies is lower. So it is all the more critical to translate these average levels of support into a more concrete understanding of the quite exceptional backing that these policies get from the public. As an example, we pick education maintenance grants for students. Approximately 70 percent assign a score of 8 or higher (where the highest possible score is 10) to the importance of the state financing education maintenance grants. In contrast, only 3 percent give it a score of less than 5. By any reasonable standard, the core policies of the welfare state enjoy overwhelming support and confront negligible opposition.

The Scandinavian (or social democratic) welfare states are *universal* welfare states.[16] In this context, universal means that citizens enjoy the right to crucial welfare benefits regardless of need. In Denmark, all have a right to receive education, health care, age-related pensions, and children allowance regardless of their financial circumstances. Yet some programs are needs tested. Social welfare in particular is provided to individuals who lack any alternative sources of income (including using their savings, selling their property, etc.). And in contrast to truly universal policies, there is a political divide over needs-tested policies. Table 3.2 shows a division on the left and right over whether it is also the obligation of the government to take care of urban renewal,

---

[16] Esping-Andersen 1990; van Kersbergen and Vis 2014.

TABLE 3.2 Importance of Welfare Services on Political Conflict Policies by Party

How important is government financing to the following?	All		Left wing		Social Liberals		Social Democrats		Center-Right		Danish People's Party	
	Median	Mode	Median	Mode	Median	Mode	Median	Mode	Median	Mode	Median	Mode
Social welfare benefits for persons outside the labor market	7	10	8	10	8	8	7	10	6	5	6	5
Family allowance benefits for families with many children	7	8	8	10	7	8	8	10	7	5	5	5
Urban renewal projects in run-down residential areas	6	5	8	8	6	5	7	8	6	5	6	5
"Start Help" for refugees	7	10	8	10	8	10	7	10	6	5	5	5

Note: Support is measured on a scale from 0 through 10. Higher values indicate greater support. Question wording: "I would now like to hear what you think about whether the government should be financing the following areas. Please use a scale from 0 to 10, where 0 indicates that it is not an area that the government should attend to, and 10 indicates that it is an area that is very important for the government to attend to. Should the government finance . . . ?"

or provide support to families whose only special need is that they have many children

It is hard to imagine a politics in which the Left is not more supportive of assistance to the poor than the Right. On a closer look, though, what is striking (at any rate to a US eye) is the muted character of the conflict between the Left and Right. So far from an implacable opponent, the Center-Right takes a middle position, even on policies that might seem to be natural candidates for ideological opposition—for example, social welfare benefits for persons outside the labor market. Even on policies where welfare and immigrants intersect—for instance, "Start Help" for refugees—although naturally less supportive of spending government money, the median score for a supporter of the Center-Right (on a scale from 0 to 10) is 6. Even Danish People's Party voters are hardly staffing the barricades; their median score is 5. We do not want to minimize the difference between the levels of support for central welfare state services and services that may disproportionately benefit immigrants. We do want to observe that services for immigrants hardly face a tidal wave of opposition.

A concern that support for the welfare state is evaporating gets things the wrong way around, at least in Denmark. As figure 3.1 reveals, public support for the central welfare services—like spending on universal public health care and help for the elderly—has been consistently high over the last two decades, and support for spending on education has consistently increased over the same period of time. The thin dotted line in the figure might provide the most soul-searching result—at least for those in the United States. Would Danes prefer lower taxes? No, they would prefer instead increased welfare services. When the Social Democrats held office during the 1990s, at least one out of every two had a preference for more welfare; since the Center-Right took over government with a proposal to not raise taxes, the pro-welfare (and by implication, pro-taxes) proportion climbed to nearly three out of every four in the electorate taken as a whole (i.e., including center-right voters). A stronger indication of support for the welfare state is difficult to imagine.

The results in tables 3.1 and 3.2 as well as figure 3.1 are thus consistent with common sense: societal consensus to a high degree on the canonical components of the welfare state; ideological cleavage to a

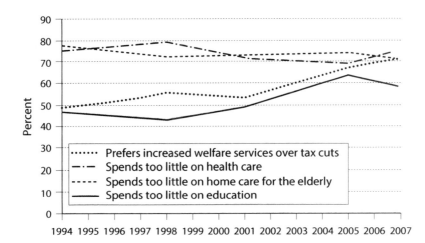

FIGURE 3.1. Welfare Attitudes over Time

Note: The figure shows percent support for welfare services over tax cuts and for three specific welfare programs. Question wording: "If in the longer run it becomes possible to lower taxes, what would you prefer? A: Lower taxes; or B: improved public services?"; "I shall read some public tasks to you, and I will ask you for each of these tasks to say whether you think the public uses too much money, a suitable amount, or too little money on these tasks: health care; home care for the elderly; education." *Source*: Danish National Election Study.

moderate degree over policies more peripheral to the core of the welfare state or benefits targeted for immigrants. Over a longer run, concern about the sapping of the popular foundations of the welfare state may be justified. A concern in the here and now about a sapping of support for the welfare state underrates the force of pride while also misconstruing the logic of resentment. For a Dane, the welfare state is an ideal of society. It may not be a uniquely Danish ideal but it is a quintessentially Danish one. Yes, many Danes believe that immigrants are taking advantage of the welfare state.[17] That may be a reason to oppose providing benefits for "them." But it is in no way a reason to oppose providing benefits for "us."

A concern about sustaining the legitimacy of the welfare state in the face of perceived violations of its principles by immigrants is

[17] In our study, 49 percent agree that "many immigrants have come to Denmark to exploit our social system," as against 37 percent who disagree.

understandable; at some future point it may be justified; but as our results have shown, that time has not yet come. Yet there is a deep, paradoxical problem beneath the surface. The moral premises under-pinning the welfare state both promote equal treatment of immigrants and open the door to discrimination against them.

THE COVENANT PARADOX

A social covenant undergirds the welfare state. This covenant rests on two interlocking propositions. First, all members of the national com-munity, by virtue of being members, have a claim to the support of the larger society. But second, and reciprocally, again by virtue of being members of the national community, all have a duty to support the welfare state. Society has an obligation to its members. Its obligation to them, though, is conditional on their honoring their duty to it.

Duty is a heavy-breathing concept. What specific logic is at work when it comes to judgments of when a person is and is not entitled to welfare assistance? Two points are essential, we believe. The first is that duty is not merely a synonym for intention. Yes, members of the national community must make an honest effort to take care of their needs and take responsibility for their lives. But this is the thin conception of duty in a context like the United States. The welfare state calls instead for a thick conception of duty—thick, moreover, in a quite specific sense. Personal sacrifice is called for. Consider this: in the United States, it is taken for granted that someone with a high school degree will own a car; a comparatively punishing level of taxa-tion makes a new car a highly expensive luxury item for many Danes with a PhD.[18] A willingness to pay a high level of taxes, in this context, is not an expression of philanthropic generosity. It is a matter of carry-ing out a duty.

The second all-important point about duty in the context of the wel-fare state is the temporal relationship between duties and rights. Ful-filling one's duty to the larger society is a condition of claiming one's rights from it. The sequencing of duties and rights is a key to the logic

---

[18] New cars are taxed 105 percent of a car's value up until seventy-nine thousand Danish kroners (roughly fifteen thousand US dollars) and then 180 percent of the value above that limit. On top of this, there is the regular Danish value-added tax of 25 percent.

of normative judgments of "deservingness."[19] Two quite different types of deservingness judgments can be brought into play. One is prospective, and the other is retrospective. The result is a paradox—the covenant paradox, we call it. On the one side, the moral premises of the welfare state work to assure equal treatment for young immigrants; on the other side, the very same premises open the door to discrimination against older immigrants.

Prospective Judgments and Equal Treatment

Consider the logic of claims for assistance by immigrants who are young and currently on welfare. They manifestly have the same duty as a native Dane to contribute to the welfare of the larger society. And there is more than one reason for seeing young immigrants get off to a good start. There are prosocial reasons, such as sympathy for their circumstances, humanitarian concern for their well-being, and appreciation of their abilities and talents. Yet whatever the specific reasons, there is a reason common to all—indeed, common even to those who do not feel especially sympathetic to immigrants, or even dislike and disdain them all in all. The issue is what young immigrants will do, not what they already have done. On the one hand, they have not yet shown themselves to be undeserving of help. On the other hand, if they do not get help, they are all too likely to fail. Failing to help them is self-defeating. The logic of prospective judgments thus works in favor of the equal treatment of immigrants and native Danes.

To test our claim about a connection between prospective judgments and equal treatment, we focus on the responsibility of the state to provide its members with resources to improve the quality of their lives. In designing an experimental test, we have been guided by two criteria. For one, our concern is with the fairness of application of welfare state programs to immigrants. So the issue of benefit and duty must matter as much applied to a young Dane as to a young immigrant. Still, it is important to formulate a claim that has an aspect specifically aimed at activating a negative stereotype of immigrant minorities.

---

[19] For standard treatments of the concept of "deservingness," see Gilens 1999; Larsen 2006; Petersen 2012; Petersen, Slothuus, Stubager, and Togeby 2011b; Sniderman, Hagen, Tetlock, and Brady 1986; van Oorschot 2000.

TABLE 3.3 Young Mother Experiment: Support for Providing Extra Help with Child Care by Party

Party	Young mother (N = 536)	Young immigrant mother (N = 515)
Overall mean	0.92	0.88
	(0.01)	(0.01)
Left wing	0.95	0.93
	(0.02)	(0.02)
Social Liberals	0.92	0.88
	(0.03)	(0.03)
Social Democrats	0.95	0.88
	(0.01)	(0.02)
Center-Right	0.92	0.88
	(0.01)	(0.02)
Danish People's Party	0.90	0.79
	(0.04)	(0.06)

Note: Entries are mean support for providing extra help with child care, measured on a 0–1 scale, with standard errors in parentheses. Higher values indicate greater support for providing extra help. Question wordings: [Young immigrant mother:] "Imagine a young mother with an immigrant background who is currently on welfare. To what extent do you agree or disagree that she should receive special help with child care so that she can begin an education program?" [Young mother:] "Imagine a young mother, who is currently on welfare. To what extent do you agree or disagree that she should receive special help with child care so that she can begin an education program?" The response categories were: agree completely, agree somewhat, neither agree nor disagree, disagree somewhat, or disagree completely. "Don't know" responses are excluded.

The "young mother" experiment meets both criteria. The respondents are told of a young mother. She needs *special* help with child care, they are informed, so that she can begin an education program. She is also, the respondents are told, "currently on welfare." The question is, then, whether she should be given the special help.[20] The experimental treatment consists of telling a randomly selected half of the respondents that this woman has "an immigrant background."

Do native Danes treat an immigrant minority as well as they treat a fellow native Dane? Table 3.3 displays the (mean) levels of support for extra help, first for the baseline condition, and then for the treatment condition. In addition. to speak to the question of whether a societal

[20] The response categories are: agree completely, agree somewhat, neither agree nor disagree, disagree somewhat, disagree completely, or don't know.

consensus is in fact society-wide, the responses of supporters of each of the major party blocs are presented. The result is clear-cut, and in truth even more so than we had anticipated.

Consider, for a start, the responses to the young woman who is (presumptively) a native Dane. She receives virtually unanimous support: the mean score is 0.92 out of a maximum possible score of 1. And she receives this level of support across the ideological spectrum. None of this is surprising; all of it is consistent with the continuing strength of the public commitment to the welfare state. What may be startling—certainly, what should be surprising to those who insist on the power of xenophobia—is the level of support for special help for the young woman explicitly identified as an immigrant. The levels of support for the woman with an immigrant background (0.88) and for native Danes (0.92) are nearly indistinguishable.

Nearly is a word that is capable of setting off alarm bells. So we present the results in more detail. For supporters of left-wing parties, the levels of support for the young woman are visually identical to those for the young woman with an immigrant background (0.95 and 0.93, respectively). For supporters of the other mainstream parties—those of the Social Liberal Party, Social Democrats, and Center-Right—the levels of support are substantively interchangeable (0.92 and 0.88) for each of the three. For adherents of the Danish People's Party, the levels of support for the two young women are not statistically different, though visually they are distinctly different (0.90 versus 0.79, respectively). Statistical significance is only a convention, and sometimes a misleading one, as we suspect it is here. The failure to clear the customary hurdle of $p < 0.05$ can reasonably be chalked up to the small numbers in the two cells.[21] Yet the primary lesson remains the same: support for special assistance for young mothers with an immigrant background is high, even in an avowedly anti-immigration party.

The young mother experiment yields two intertwined findings. First, the societal consensus in support of the welfare state remains strong. Second, support for welfare state assistance is as forthcoming for immigrants as it is for native citizens. In light of widespread concern about xenophobia, it is no small matter to see that Danes—across the political

---

[21] The N for the Danish People's Party supporters in the young mother condition is 42; in the young mother with an immigrant background, it is 35.

spectrum—give equal treatment to appeals for welfare assistance to immigrants as to their fellow Danes.

Getting a helping hand from the state is one side of the social covenant. Fulfilling one's responsibilities to the larger society is the other. In the current climate of opinion, it is surely reasonable to believe that Danes will impose stricter requirements to find a job on immigrant minorities than on fellow Danes. Indeed, because it is reasonable to believe this notion, our claim of the evenhandedness of prospective judgments should be put to a further and, if possible, stiffer test.

In the 1990s, as a complement to the welfare state's duties to citizens, a policy was introduced to condition welfare and unemployment benefits on the duties of citizens to the welfare state.[22] This policy, commonly referred to as the activation policy, includes the obligation to meet certain requirements, such as taking temporary jobs, or fulfilling courses and "job training" to facilitate finding a regular job. These temporary jobs are typically dull and sometimes meaningless. So, too, are some of the job training courses that citizens are required to take. The requirements are more demanding for people under the age of thirty; in fact, individuals under the age of thirty can be forced to begin an education if they want to retain their financial support from the government. The arguments made by the political Right for the activation policy emphasized that its aim was to motivate people to help themselves. Strategic or otherwise, this contention puts a person in an ideal position to say, "I'm being tough on you for your own good." The activation policy therefore opens up an obvious opportunity for Danes to be punitive in its application to immigrant minorities.

The "tougher requirements" experiment focuses on young men on welfare. Specifically, the respondents are asked, "Imagine a young man currently on welfare. To what extent do you agree or disagree that the activation requirements for him should be made stricter?"[23] Half the time, the recipient was described as "a young man currently on welfare." The other half he was depicted as "a young man with an immigrant background currently on welfare."

---

[22] For further discussion, see Cox 2001; Loftager 2004, 93–95.

[23] Following our standard practice, the response alternatives are: agree completely, agree somewhat, neither agree nor disagree, disagree somewhat, disagree completely, or don't know.

Table 3.4 displays the levels of support for making requirements to receive welfare payments tougher for young men. The first point that we would like to make is that the results mimic the actual political debate over the activation policy's introduction. The Social Democrats introduced the policy with broad support across much of the ideological spectrum, albeit in the face of some opposition from the left wing—especially the Red-Green Alliance—which views tougher regulations for receiving benefits as a betrayal of the welfare state. So we see in the first column, which reports responses in the control condition, that the one exception to consensual support for a tougher activation policy—and it is only a partial exception—appears on the left wing. Paralleling the ideological debate over the need to make the welfare state more efficient, we also see that support for tougher requirements to qualify for welfare payments increases as one moves from left to right on the ideological spectrum. Both of these aspects of the results speak to the validity of the tougher requirements experiment.

The question that the experiment was designed to answer was whether there is a double standard. Are Danes more likely to favor tougher requirements when the beneficiaries are immigrants than when they are fellow Danes? The results in table 3.4 speak directly to this question.

Compare the levels of support when the young man is not described as an immigrant (the control condition, column 1) and when he is characterized as an immigrant (the treatment condition, column 2). For the Social Democrats, support for tougher requirements in the control condition is 0.76, and it is 0.75 in the treatment condition—in a word, in favor of evenhanded treatment. For the left wing, the numbers are 0.68 and 0.69, respectively, again expressing evenhanded treatment of immigrant minorities and fellow citizens. And offering another example of what is obvious ex post but not obvious ex ante, supporters of the Danish People's Party come down hard on stricter requirements for immigrants to receive welfare payments, yet they come down just as hard on their fellow Danes. The numbers in the native Dane and immigrant minority conditions are 0.88 and 0.84, respectively.

Moreover, the quantitative results display a modest wobbliness that—for experienced data analysts—is reassuring. For supporters of all parties except the left wing, support for tougher requirements is higher for fellow Danes than for immigrants. On its face, it is bizarre

TABLE 3.4 Tougher Requirements Experiment with Young Man: Support for Tougher Requirements for Receiving Welfare Payments by Party

Party	Young man (N = 329)	Young immigrant man (N = 333)
Overall mean	0.79	0.75
	(0.02)	(0.02)
Left wing	0.68	0.69
	(0.07)	(0.06)
Social Liberals	0.76	0.64
	(0.06)	(0.06)
Social Democrats	0.76	0.75
	(0.04)	(0.04)
Center-Right	0.84	0.78
	(0.03)	(0.03)
Danish People's Party	0.88	0.84
	(0.05)	(0.07)

Note: Entries are mean support for tougher requirements for receiving welfare payments, measured on a 0–1 scale, with standard errors in parentheses. Higher values indicate greater support for tougher requirements. Question wordings: [Young man:] "Imagine a young man currently on welfare. To what extent do you agree or disagree that the activation requirement for him should be made stricter?" [Young immigrant man:] "Imagine a young man with an immigrant background who is currently on welfare. To what extent do you agree or disagree that the activation requirement for him should be made stricter?" The response categories were: agree completely, agree somewhat, neither agree nor disagree, disagree somewhat, or disagree completely. "Don't know" responses are excluded.

to observe Danes applying a tougher standard to fellow Danes than immigrant minorities. Happily, closer inspection of the results makes it plain that this anomalous result is an arithmetic illusion. The apparent differences are not statistically significant. As the standard errors demonstrate, Danes treat fellow Danes and immigrant minorities alike.

The young mother and tougher requirements experiments thus tell a mutually reinforcing tale: Danes treating immigrants and fellows the same. It would be splendid if this were the end of the story. But if it were the end, this would not be a story. It would be a fable.

Retrospective Judgments and Discriminatory Treatment

The covenant paradox is grounded in the linkage of rights to duties. Not all claims to benefits are connected to duties. Citizens do not forfeit medical attention and assistance even if they have not lived exemplary lives—even if their lives have fallen far short of exemplary. But what sustains the welfare state as a provider of services is a social covenant. Society has an obligation to its members. Its members, though, also have an obligation to society. They must do their best to take care of their own needs.

It would nevertheless mock the meaning of citizens' obligations in a welfare society to reduce them to a duty of self-reliance. The covenant that underpins the welfare state has a larger compass. All have a duty to contribute to the welfare of all. To be sure, because of differences in talent and opportunity, it is a fact of life that some contribute more than others, and some benefit more than others. Yet citizens are not capable of being moral mathematicians, distributing benefits in proportion to a calculus of contributions. If they wish, however, they can take advantage of rules of thumb to judge whether others are indeed making an effort.

Again, our argument rests on a solid foundation of previous work. A large literature from various disciplines shows that in making judgments about who deserves government aid or who in everyday life deserves assistance, a major standard is "making an effort."[24] Making an effort is in one respect a modest standard, and in this sense, an accommodating one. Who can credibly declare that a young immigrant, just starting out in school or a career, is bound to fall short of the mark? When applied to older immigrants, the same standard, making an effort, opens the door to discrimination.[25]

Purely as a matter of fact, many immigrant women have never attempted to join the labor force.[26] From the perspective of a traditional or religious culture, there are good reasons for this, but they are not good ones from a contemporary Danish perspective. Insofar as immigrant women meet the expectations that immigrants coming from traditionalist cultures have of women, they fail to meet those that Danes have of women, immigrant or not. And just as a class of judgments

[24] Feather 2006; Weiner 1995; Zak 2007; Petersen 2012.

[25] Retrospective evaluations typically can be based on less ambiguous cues of the effort of welfare recipients because there is more past behavior to use in assessing welfare recipients. As we have demonstrated elsewhere, such clearer cues, in turn, more easily fit the deservingness heuristic and hence will more likely guide welfare policy opinion (Petersen et al. 2011b).

[26] Pedersen 2011, 12. That said, employment rates among non-Western immigrants have been growing in recent years, also among women.

about who deserves help are forward-looking or prospective, because they are being made about young people, so is there a counterbalancing class that are backward-looking or retrospective, because they are being made about older people.

The tougher requirements experiment was designed to investigate retrospective as well as prospective judgments. A set of randomly selected respondents were asked whether the activation requirement should be made stricter for a woman in her fifties who is currently on welfare and has "an immigrant background." The respondents randomly assigned to the control condition were asked exactly the same question except no mention was made of having an immigrant background.[27] Older immigrants have had an opportunity to show that they are meeting their obligation to work and make an effort to take care of themselves. But it is doubly easy for anyone who wants to punish an immigrant to take the position that they have failed to meet their obligation to the larger society. It is doubly easy, first, because there is a widely held stereotype of Muslim women being restricted to the home, and second, because this stereotype has some grounding in reality, judged by the low workforce participation rates of Muslim women. The result: characterizing one of the women as an immigrant calls to mind a picture of many immigrant women who are opting out of their duties. Just as encountering a Danish woman in her fifties receiving welfare benefits would give the impression that she lost her job, encountering an immigrant woman in the same situation raises suspicions that she never had a job.

Table 3.5 displays the reactions, overall and by party, of the respondents to an older woman under immigrant and nonimmigrant conditions. There manifestly is more support for imposing tougher requirements for receiving welfare support on immigrant women (0.57) than on fellow Danes (0.45). As important, a double standard is evident across the political spectrum. Thus, the mean level of support for imposing tougher requirements for supporters of left-wing parties when the woman is an immigrant is 0.56, compared to 0.37 when she is not. For Social Democrats, comparable numbers are 0.56 and 0.35, respectively. For adherents of the Danish People's Party, the numbers are 0.67 compared to 0.38.[28]

---

[27] The response categories were, of course, as mentioned above.

[28] It would not be wise to attach too much importance to interparty differences in light of the relatively small numbers.

TABLE 3.5 Tougher Requirements Experiment with Woman in Her Fifties: Support for Tougher Requirements for Receiving Welfare Payments by Party

Party	Woman in her fifties (N = 340)	Immigrant woman in her fifties (N = 331)
Overall mean	0.45	0.57
	(0.02)	(0.02)
Left wing	0.37	0.56
	(0.07)	(0.06)
Social Liberals	0.46	0.54
	(0.07)	(0.07)
Social Democrats	0.35	0.56
	(0.04)	(0.05)
Center-Right	0.51	0.61
	(0.04)	(0.04)
Danish People's Party	0.38	0.67
	(0.07)	(0.07)

Note: Entries are mean support for tougher requirements for receiving welfare payments, measured on a 0–1 scale, with standard errors in parentheses. Higher values indicate greater support for tougher requirements. Question wordings: [Woman in her fifties:] "Imagine a woman in her fifties who is currently on welfare. To what extent do you agree or disagree that the activation requirement for her should be made stricter?" [Immigrant woman in her fifties:] "Imagine a woman in her fifties with an immigrant background who is currently on welfare. To what extent do you agree or disagree that the activation requirement for her should be made stricter?" The response categories were: agree completely, agree somewhat, neither agree nor disagree, disagree somewhat, or disagree completely. "Don't know" responses are excluded.

This is a downpayment on evidence in support of our theory of retrospective versus prospective evaluations. We have more proof to offer, though. On our account, retrospective judgments open the door to judgments that immigrants have not lived up to their end of the social covenant. Accordingly, we focus here on judgments about the level of benefits to which families with many children are entitled. All the respondents in the "many children" experiment are asked to imagine a family "where both the mother and father are on welfare."[29] Then they are asked to what extent they agree or disagree that "their welfare

---

[29] The sample as a whole was partitioned. Half of the respondents (randomly selected) participated in the young mother experiment, and the other half in the many children experiment.

should be reduced in order to push them to find a job."[30] One randomly selected set is told that this is "an immigrant family with many children"; the other is told only that it is "a family with many children."

It is our claim that retrospective judgments on whether a person deserves assistance provide more room for unfavorable evaluations. Those who think ill of immigrants will be disposed to infer that an immigrant couple in the many children experiment has not made an effort to contribute to the larger society but instead has chosen to stay at home and collect social benefits.

Table 3.6 presents reactions to immigrant and nonimmigrant families with many children. Again, a double standard is undeniable. For the electorate as a whole, the mean score (from 0 to 1) in favor of cutting welfare benefits when the family is identified as having an immigrant background is 0.52, as compared to 0.41 for a Danish family with many children. The disparity in the treatment of immigrants does not, to judge from the results in table 3.6, run the political gamut. For those on the left, the differences are either statistically insignificant or substantively insignificant, once standard errors are taken into account. Only when one moves away from the liberal Left can one be confident that immigrants are treated differently and worse. For Social Democrats, the mean score for cutting welfare benefits for immigrant families with many children is 0.46, compared to 0.33 for a similar Danish family. For the Center-Right and Danish People's Party, the comparable numbers are 0.67 versus 0.52, and 0.72 versus 0.53, respectively.

Why this difference between the two experiments? A conjecture that comes to mind is that the policy in the second experiment affects children, and as such, those on the left may respond with more sympathy to an immigrant family than they otherwise would. An alternative conjecture is that there is indeed a difference between the political Left and the Center-Right. This is a plausible speculation. The farther to the left citizens are on the political spectrum, the more favorable their attitudes are toward immigrants.[31] But the major conclusion to draw from

---

[30] The response categories are, again, as noted above.

[31] The correlation between the measure of attitudes toward immigrants (high scores being more negative) and partisan-ideological orientation is r = 0.45. The argument justifying the term *positive* can be found in our discussion of inclusive tolerance (see chapter 5), but we do want to note that only the left-wing and Social Liberal parties could be said to fall on the positive side of the attitudes toward immigrants scale (with mean scores of

TABLE 3.6 Many Children Experiment: Support for Cutting Welfare Benefits by Party

Party	Family with many children (N = 490)	Immigrant family with many children (N = 462)
Overall mean	0.41	0.52
	(0.02)	(0.02)
Left wing	0.19	0.25
	(0.04)	(0.05)
Social Liberals	0.30	0.27
	(0.05)	(0.05)
Social Democrats	0.33	0.46
	(0.04)	(0.04)
Center-Right	0.52	0.67
	(0.03)	(0.03)
Danish People's Party	0.53	0.72
	(0.06)	(0.06)

Note: Entries are mean support for cutting welfare payments, measured on a 0–1 scale, with standard errors in parentheses. Higher values indicate cutting welfare payments. Question wordings: [Family with many children:] "Imagine a family with many children, where both the mother and father are on welfare. To what extent do you agree or disagree that their welfare should be reduced in order to push them to find a job?" [Immigrant family with many children:] "Imagine an immigrant family with many children, where both the mother and father are on welfare. To what extent do you agree or disagree that their welfare should be reduced in order to push them to find a job?" The response categories were: agree completely, agree somewhat, neither agree nor disagree, disagree somewhat, or disagree completely. "Don't know" responses are excluded.

the two experiments goes to the heart of the matter. The many children experiment, like the tougher requirements experiment, shows that the public practices a discriminatory double standard, treating immigrants differently and worse than fellow Danes.

Two Critical Assumptions

These findings carry us some distance, but not quite across the goal line. Two crucial assumptions demand examination. The first is that we have presumed that people who are not identified as immigrants

---

0.31 and 0.30, respectively, on a scale ranging from 0 to 1, with 0.50 as the midpoint). The comparable scores for Social Democrats, the Center-Right, and the Danish People's Party are 0.47, 0.55, and 0.75, respectively.

are taken to be Danes. Perhaps this is true, yet perhaps it is only partly true, or possibly not true at all. What if, hearing that a person is on welfare, the respondents automatically infer that the person is an immigrant. After all, it is not merely that many in the majority perceive immigrants to be exploiting welfare. Immigrant minorities in fact are—and are widely known to be—overrepresented on welfare rolls.[32] In eastern Denmark, for example, immigrants from non-Western countries make up 31 percent of all recipients of social welfare, even though they constitute only 8 percent of the population.[33] Is it not possible—indeed, more than just possible—that our respondents think "immigrant" when they hear "on welfare"? And insofar as they do, our assumption that the experiments are providing a window to differential reactions toward immigrant minorities and fellow Danes falls to the ground.

The second critical assumption is subtler. Grant the findings of previous experiments that Danes respond more favorably to fellow Danes than to immigrant minorities when making retrospective judgments. The question is why? Does it have something to do with the moral compass that underpins the welfare state? Or is it for some other reason, such as a sense of a shared national identity?

To pry out answers to these questions, we turn to another policy debate. From 2001 to 2011, the center-right government was in office, and during this time introduced a bundle of policies to restrict welfare benefits, with the objective of increasing the number of immigrants who are working rather than on welfare. Specifically, the "450 hours rule" requires that for either member of a married couple to receive welfare benefits, *both* the husband and wife need to have had paid work for at least 450 hours over the last two years. The argument for the 450 hours rule is partly the familiar one that "now it actually pays for them to find a job," as the then-minister of employment, Inger Støjberg, declared. But it was also combined with an assertion less common in this context—namely, equality for women. As Støjberg went on to say, "In particular many women have been able to use this rule

[32] Schultz-Nielsen, Gerdes, and Wadensjö 2011.
[33] Beskæftigelsesregion Hovedstaden og Sjælland 2009.

to persuade their husband that they should be allowed to take a job; otherwise the family would lose its income."[34]

Another "reformist" policy to increase the efficiency of the welfare state was putting a "ceiling" on welfare benefits. The center-right government contended that this would increase economic incentives to get off the welfare rolls.[35] Its premise: the smaller the difference between social welfare benefits and the minimum wage, the weaker the motivation to get off welfare; the larger the difference, the stronger the motivation. The then-minister of employment, Claus Hjort Frederiksen (later the minister of finance), was prominent in the debate over the initiation—and later defense—of a welfare ceiling policy. "We have to arrange our social system in a way that always provides an incentive to take a job," he argued, going on to say, "We do welfare recipients a disservice if we don't try to find them a job. . . . [With the ceiling,] we offer an incentive so that even a little extra effort will pay off."[36]

Implemented in 2004, the policy imposed a ceiling on how much a person may receive in overall benefits from the welfare state (including social welfare, housing, and some additional benefits like help to families with children). This cap on benefits kicks in once a recipient has been on welfare for six months or more. In addition, if both the husband and wife are on welfare, a still-lower ceiling is imposed on the welfare benefits. In the early phases of the debate over the ceiling policy, explicit references to immigrants on welfare were rare.[37] Subsequently, the linkage has become explicit. We accordingly chose to focus on the ceiling policy.

[34] "Flere indvandrere i arbejde" 2010.

[35] All along the way, however, the Danish People's Party was aware of the implications for immigrants on welfare. While they were reluctant to support the welfare reform in the first place, that doubt vanished once it became clear in statistics from the Ministry of Employment that nearly three out of four families hit by the ceiling on welfare would be immigrant families. "When we saw these figures," leading Member of Parliament Kristian Thulesen Dahl said, "we no longer had any doubt. They show that it is immigrants in particular who suck welfare money. To an extent bordering on abuse. Therefore, it is important to ensure they have an incentive to work" ("Loft over kontanthjælpen" 2002). In September 2012, Dahl was appointed chair of the Danish People's Party, succeeding Pia Kjærsgaard.

[36] "De svage hårdt presset af reform" 2003; "Lavere kontanthjælp skal få folk i job" 2004.

[37] Many of these policies have subsequently been repealed by the center-left government that took office in 2011.

The purpose of the ceiling experiment is twofold. One objective is to answer the question of whether Danes reflexively think of immigrants when they learn that a person is on welfare. The other is to shed light on why Danes support welfare assistance. Concerning one of the three conditions of the ceiling experiment, we asked a randomized set of respondents: "There has been debate about a ceiling on social welfare benefits, which reduces the benefits for couples where both depend on social welfare benefits. As you might know, some people are against this ceiling on social welfare benefits. What do you think? Should the ceiling on social benefits be maintained or should it be rescinded?"

This is, of course, the baseline condition. Just as in previous experiments, we asked another set of respondents exactly the same question apart from one difference. The interviewer presented an argument against the policy based on immigrants' needs.[38] Specifically, the second sentence of the question read: "As you might know, some people are against this ceiling on social welfare benefits, *because it hits immigrants in particular, thereby hurting integration.*"[39]

Table 3.7 displays the reactions of our respondents depending on whether they were presented with the "hurts immigrants" claim (on the right) or not (on the left). When the argument against the policy is that it will hurt immigrants, the mean level of support for a ceiling on benefits is 0.65; when no assertion at all is made, the mean is 0.55 ($p < 0.05$). Straightforwardly, this is a discriminatory double standard: there is more support when it is made explicit that immigrants will pay the price of the policy, and less when it is not.

We previously put two conjectures on the table to account for evenhandedness on the part of the left-wing and Social Liberal parties in the many children experiment. Perhaps it had to do with the proposed welfare cuts hurting children, and perhaps with these parties' broad outlook on politics. If the first is correct, we should not see evenhandedness on the left in the ceiling experiment, since there is no explicit reference to the fate of children. If the second is right, we should see evenhandedness on the left, since the broad outlook of the left-wing

---

[38] This is a highly realistic contention as two out of every three individuals affected by the ceiling on welfare benefits were immigrants; almost everyone hit by the "300 hours rule" were immigrants (Pedersen 2011, 24).

[39] Emphasis added.

TABLE 3.7 Ceiling Experiment: Hurt Immigrants by Party

Party	No reason given (N = 277)	Hurt immigrants (N = 243)
Overall mean	0.55	0.65
	(0.02)	(0.03)
Left wing	0.31	0.35
	(0.06)	(0.08)
Social Liberals	0.47	0.45
	(0.06)	(0.09)
Social Democrats	0.44	0.56
	(0.05)	(0.06)
Center-Right	0.68	0.76
	(0.04)	(0.04)
Danish People's Party	0.74	0.86
	(0.07)	(0.05)

Note: Entries are mean support for a ceiling on welfare benefits, measured on a 0–1 scale, with standard errors in parentheses. Higher values indicate greater support for tougher requirements. Question wordings: [No reason given:] "There has been debate about a ceiling on social welfare benefits, which reduces the benefits for couples where both depend on social welfare benefits. As you might know, some people are against this ceiling on social welfare benefits. What do you think? Should the ceiling on social benefits be maintained or should it be rescinded?" [Hurt immigrants:] "There has been debate about a ceiling on social welfare benefits, which reduces the benefits for couples, where both depend on social welfare benefits. As you might know, some people are against this ceiling on social welfare benefits, because it hits immigrants in particular, thereby hurting integration. What do you think? Should the ceiling on social benefits be maintained or should it be rescinded?" The response options in maintaining or rescinding the ceiling on social welfare benefits were: agree or agree somewhat. "Don't know" responses are excluded.

party on politics is as relevant to the policy question raised by the ceiling experiment as in the many children experiment. In fact, as an inspection of table 3.7 shows, consistent with the political outlook speculation, the Left is evenhanded in both experiments.

The ideological conjecture remains a conjecture all the same, since the Left displayed a discriminatory double standard in the tougher requirements experiment. The conclusion to draw—and one in which we have confidence—is that in the society as a whole, there is a clear pattern of discrimination in the application of policy: the public is both more likely to impose more demanding standards on older immigrants to qualify for welfare benefits than on their fellow citizens, when both are in the same circumstances, and less likely to approve of their receiving welfare benefits than their fellow citizens, again when both are in the same circumstances. In short, on welfare issues, older immigrants are treated differently and worse than are native Danes.

So far, our tests of discrimination have followed the same design: mention or no mention of immigrant status. The ceiling experiment included a third condition, however. In this third condition, the question included an appeal to the values of the social covenant, with the second sentence reading: "As you might know, some people are against this ceiling on social welfare benefits, *because it would hit the weakest members of society and create greater inequality.*"[40]

The pivotal comparison now is between those in the "no reason given" condition and those in the "appeal to the covenant" one.[41] Why pivotal? Because the more similar their reactions to the two conditions, the more compelling the inference that Danes truly have internalized the moral compact of the welfare state, since there is no need to call their attention to its key premise—the need to protect the weakest members of society and combat inequality.[42]

Table 3.8 compares the responses of those in no reason given and appeal to the covenant conditions. In the electorate as a whole, an appeal to the values of the social covenant is superfluous. When an appeal is made—in strong terms, it is worth remarking—to the duty to protect the weakest and fight inequality, the mean level of support for capping benefits is 0.52; when no appeal is made, the mean level of support for a cap is 0.55. The difference is neither substantively nor statistically significant.

Examining table 3.8 in detail, for every partisan group, once standard errors are taken into account, differences between their responses in the two experimental conditions are either zero or trivial.

What should we conclude from these results? Two conclusions stand out.

---

[40] Emphasis added.

[41] The ceiling experiment in fact included three other conditions, similar to those mentioned here, except that they provided a social democratic partisan source cue. As we do not focus on elite influence here, we did not include the respondents from those conditions.

[42] This is an example of how the absence of a treatment effect can provide evidence for a substantive hypothesis. For a related discussion, see Sniderman 2011.

TABLE 3.8 Ceiling Experiment: Appeal to the Covenant by Party

Party	No reason given (N = 277)	Appeal to the covenant (N = 283)
Overall mean	0.55	0.52
	(0.02)	(0.03)
Left wing	0.31	0.22
	(0.06)	(0.05)
Social Liberals	0.47	0.28
	(0.06)	(0.07)
Social Democrats	0.44	0.41
	(0.05)	(0.05)
Center-Right	0.68	0.67
	(0.04)	(0.03)
Danish People's Party	0.74	0.59
	(0.07)	(0.08)

Note: Entries are mean support for a ceiling on welfare benefits, measured on a 0–1 scale, with standard errors in parentheses. Higher values indicate imposing a ceiling. Question wordings: [No reason given:] "There has been debate about a ceiling on social welfare benefits, which reduces the benefits for couples when both depend on social welfare benefits. As you might know, some people are against this ceiling on social welfare benefits. What do you think? Should the ceiling on social benefits be maintained or should it be rescinded?" [Appeal to the covenant:] "There has been debate about a ceiling on social welfare benefits, which reduces the benefits for couples when both depend on social welfare benefits. As you might know, some people are against this ceiling on social welfare benefits, because it would hit the weakest members of society and create greater inequality. What do you think? Should the ceiling on social benefits be maintained or should it be rescinded?" The response options in maintaining or rescinding the ceiling on social welfare benefits were: agree or agree somewhat. "Don't know" responses are excluded.

First, opposition to a cap on welfare benefits is grounded in a commitment to the values of the welfare state—as captured by reference to inequality in the words of the experimental appeal. Second, there is a commitment to these values; they have been so deeply internalized that it is not necessary to call them to the conscious attention of Danes in order to evoke a supportive response toward those on welfare.

A SUMMARY WORD

Our objective has been to understand how the moral covenant underpinning the welfare state can generate opposing reactions to immigrants: sometimes equal treatment, and sometimes discriminatory treatment.

This is paradoxical on its face. So we have christened this the covenant paradox. What, then, is our explanation of the paradox?

The moral premises of the covenant are universal. All who are members of the national community are entitled to some specific benefits from the welfare state—such as medical care—whether or not they perform their part of the social bargain and discharge their duty to contribute to supporting the welfare state. But for many benefits, a person's claim depends on meeting their responsibility to contribute to supporting the welfare state. In turn, there is no principled ground to support the right of a native Dane to these benefits and deny the right of an immigrant to them absent a reason to believe that the latter has failed to meet their responsibility to contribute to the collective effort.

Hence the gulf between retrospective and prospective judgments. Young immigrants have not yet had an opportunity to fail to meet their duties, so they surely must be given the same opportunity to do so as fellow Danes. In contrast, older immigrants are all too likely to have failed to meet their duties—or more precisely, as we will see, to be perceived to have done so by those who bear them ill will—and as such, are less deserving of help and more in need of tough measures to get them working rather than living on welfare. The result is the covenant paradox: equal treatment for younger immigrants, and discriminatory treatment for older ones.

CHAPTER 4

Flash Point

THE IDEOLOGICAL BASES OF ANTI-IMMIGRATION POLITICS

O ur aim in this chapter is to bring to light how—and why—the ideological foundations of party systems in western Europe pose a potentially explosive threat to the inclusion of immigrants. It has, of course, long been recognized that right-wing ideological values are a major force propelling anti-immigration politics. Though by no means the only symptom, the most florid expression is the rise of radical anti-immigration parties—among others, the National Front in France, Freedom Party in the Netherlands, Flemish Interest in Belgium, and Freedom Party of Austria. A towering stack of studies of such anti-immigration parties has accumulated, and it grows higher and higher every year.[1] So we have chosen a different goal. We will concentrate all our attention on the political mainstream. We want to reveal what is happening at the center of politics, not at its extremes.

As we will show, a large pool of voters predisposed to respond to the appeals of anti-immigration parties are gathering at the political center. They have not yet become adherents of extremist parties, and it is not preordained that they will. But they have a bent of mind—an ideological outlook—that makes them susceptible to extremist appeals, and we aim to illuminate that fact. The real potential for change in the future rests with those who are presently centrists yet potential defectors to the political extremes.

---

[1] For some of the best-known studies, see, for example, Kitschelt 1995, 2007; van der Brug and Fennema 2007; Mudde 2007; Norris 2005.

The Claim

It has become an analytic reflex to pair left politics with modernism and equality, and right politics with traditionalism and hierarchy. It follows that intolerance is at odds with left-wing values and, conversely, rooted in right-wing ones. There is truth in this—indeed, a large measure of truth. It nonetheless is our claim that the political contest between the Left and Right has obscured the impact of a strain of belief shared by many on both the left and the right: communitarianism.

Communitarianism in all its forms emphasizes the role of the larger community in defining the identity of community members and establishing the values giving meaning to their lives. In turn, the communitarian ethos is built into the moral premises underpinning the welfare state: the obligation of the national community to assure the well-being of its members and its members to contribute to the well-being of the national community. Communitarianism so conceived is not a synonym for cultural conservatism. Yet it folds naturally into cultural conservatism, since the premise of both is the priority of the community over the individual. Insofar as this is so, economic egalitarianism and cultural conservatism are easily braided together to form a politically potent version of communitarianism.

Obviously enough, the combination of economic egalitarianism and cultural conservatism is under increasing strain from urbanization, secularization, globalization, and immigration, among other transforming forces. Hence our prediction: the power of culturally conservative values to propel antipathy to immigrants is galvanized when they are joined in the minds of voters with egalitarian economic values. In a word, the mixture of right-wing cultural values and left-wing economic ones is combustible.

We want to spell out the reasoning undergirding the combustibility hypothesis, and what is more, to do so in the most direct and true-to-life form.

The Past Seen from the Present, the Present Seen from the Past

To bring our ideas to life, we begin with a conversation with a man who has lived through the heyday of the Danish welfare state. He is, of course, only one individual, different in countless ways from others. But he has the advantage of being a real person, and just because his words are his own, they animate his values, memories, resentments, and above all, sense of loss. His expression of this loss is his own, but his sense of it is shared by many others, and highlights, in a way that is immediate because it is personal, the ideological dynamics of anti-immigration politics.

John

John is a seventy-three-year-old pensioner who worked at the docks in the Aarhus harbor.[2] He grew up in a rural area near Aarhus. His father was an unskilled laborer, beginning as a hod carrier and subsequently becoming a metal grinder. John graduated from the Jysk Teknologisk Institut and, after an apprenticeship, became qualified as a skilled mechanic. He has hardly ever been out of work and has three children.

John is not affiliated with the Danish People's Party: "I've always voted for the Social Democrats, and that's as far right as I go," as he puts it. His political affiliations are mainstream. At the same time, John fits the stereotypical picture of a nativist who sees Muslim immigrants as a threat to his country's national character and identity. "They take part in nothing," he insists. "They don't even learn to speak Danish when they come to live in Denmark." This is not an isolated interjection, we would emphasize. He goes on to say, "I know that many of those who come here, even though they've been here for years, they still have severe problems with the language, don't they?" Why? Because, John declares, "they are so damned marked by religion; they have that blasted religion hanging over their heads, don't they?"

"Damned" and "blasted" are stare-in-your face signs of the strength of John's feelings. But his anger and scorn are not directed at religion. Islam, for John, is a synonym for culture, not theology, and he has contempt for it. His characterization is biting as well as dismissive:

---

[2] We have chosen the name John to assure the anonymity of the interviewee. We want to express our deep appreciation to our colleague, Gitte Sommer Harrits, for making the interview transcript available to us. For her report on this project, see Harrits 2005. The interpretation of this material is strictly our own.

They talk about code of honor and things like that. It's quite extreme, isn't it? Their code of honor, right? Because one of their daughters would even think about marrying someone he has not chosen, and because the father's honor is hurt, he has to kill her; it's crazy. [And their culture is something that has] gone on for thousands of years, and they're still marked by it.

The anger and contempt in John's words are unmistakable. This is just what we would expect a nativist to say and how we would expect them to say it. And just as one would also suppose, John is concerned about the loss of Denmark's cultural identity. But what one might not expect is that in his sense of a loss of Denmark's culture, the clash of cultural values is a secondary consideration. The loss of social solidarity is the primary issue.

Early in the interview, John remarks, "Not so long ago, well, bloody hell, ten to fifteen years ago, Denmark was famous for being a homogeneous population and things like that." And why is it no longer "famous for being a homogenous population," you may ask? Not—according to John—because of the intrusion of an alien culture. The problem is quite different: it is emergence of class distinctions rather than the clash of cultures. Explaining what he means by Denmark no longer being homogeneous, John asserts, "I really think there are signs in the sun, moon, and stars that there'll be an upper class and a first class and a second class and then the rest."

The fact of class distinctions upsets John, deeply. Yet what opens a window on his values is why class distinctions matter. "It's a change of attitude because that's the way it's become, well, even my colleagues and they, well, if they see the chance, they never think that we're all in it together. As soon as something pops up, they make someone believe that now you have these advantages, and then they listen to that and then forget all about who you are." This is a remarkably revealing comment. No doubt, John counts it as a step backward that people now pursue their different economic interests. It is not a conflict, though, between those who are better off and those who are less well off that is his concern. His concern is with the loss of social solidarity, which he regards as the price, unintended but no less real for all that, of almost everyone being better off. As he proclaims in a heartfelt reflection:

As I begin to remember, from then our economic conditions have become so much better, haven't they? And we're also very much better off in 2004 than in 1970, for example. There is no doubt about it, no doubt about it. No doubt about it. And then I have to say, why is it that you talk about the time when you think it was so good and so wonderful? But, er . . . I remember our old chairman of the Danish Confederation of Trade Unions, he was on the podium in his farewell speech when he stopped. . . . He said we have won a pyrrhic victory, and perhaps he's right, because we've simply got so much, or so many expectations, you see, that people no longer feel that they're all in it together in one way or the other.

John has done his best to stand against the tide, and this includes inculcating his children with proper values and raising them to adhere to traditional standards. As he says, "I have of course raised them to behave properly." The word *properly* speaks volumes. Then, to drive home just what he means by it, John goes on to observe,

I have, damn it, raised them not to throw litter in the streets. And none of my children do so. I can see, they don't, you know. Whenever they've had an ice cream and they threw it, and then "Pick it up. Pick it up in your pocket and then in. . . ." Yeah, and then I've always said, you know, "You can do whatever you like, you can do exactly what you like, but I don't want any crap, I don't want any crap, so make out yourself how far you wanna go. If you've done something and I've given you some trouble eh," and that's the way it's been.

John's values—for people to behave properly; take responsibility not only for their own property but also the public's; be clean and orderly; "not to throw litter in the street"; and insist on respect from their children ("You can do whatever you like . . . but I don't want any crap")—are the values of a cultural conservative. His overriding theme all the same is the loss of "having a feeling of community," people instead standing behind their "private hedge," and "our society [changing] from being what I regarded as a fairly equal society [to becoming] a grab bag."

What are we hearing when John talks like this? Not the past itself but rather the past viewed from the present—memories of life as a child when his family had scarcely anything; as a young boy moving from adolescence to adulthood finding his vocation and acquiring his skills; as a parent instructing his children on the standards they should live by; and as a man in the last cycle of his life, retired, viewing the world as it is now through the mirror of his recollections of the way it was and his beliefs about the way it should be. Was he as happy then as he now says he was? Was he as convinced of the reality of the feeling of community when he was raising his family, peering into an unknown and ineluctably uncertain future that he now believes in? Answers to these questions are unknowable and for our purposes beside the point. What matters is not what was in fact so, or even what John long ago believed was so, but instead what he now believes to have been so.

We have endeavored to hear John as though he were standing in front of us. What strikes us most forcefully is his feeling of being simultaneously assaulted on two fronts. The values of the Left—equality and a feeling of community—are under attack. So, too, are those of the Right—behaving properly. This feeling of being attacked concurrently on two fronts produces, we contend, an explosive reaction against immigration and immigrants. We call this claim the combustibility hypothesis, and believe it is key to a fuller account of the ideological bases of anti-immigration politics.

Ideological Politics

To show what the combustibility hypothesis adds to what is already known, we begin by setting out the standard model of the ideological structure of Danish (and more broadly, western European) politics. Our objectives are threefold. The first is to show that our study provides strong support for the standard two-dimensional model of ideological politics in general and the ideological basis of anti-immigration politics in particular. Our second objective is to demonstrate that the standard model is incomplete. It is necessary to take account of the explosive interaction of economic egalitarianism and cultural conservatism. Having demonstrated—and replicated—this empirically, our third objective is to embed our findings in a broader theoretical context.

The Ideological Bases of Anti-immigration Politics

Politics in western Europe, it is widely agreed, is organized around two ideological dimensions.[3] The first and historically dominant one revolves around economic redistribution. The specific issues that make up this left-right dimension naturally vary with time and place. The basic logic of the underlying conflict, however, has been remarkably stable. In Denmark, the ideological Left's overarching goal has been the reduction of economic inequality. It has principally used the state's power to impose highly progressive taxation and strong constraints on private enterprise as a means to establish the welfare state as well as reduce the inequality of not merely economic opportunity but also economic conditions.[4] The contemporary ideological Right has accepted the legitimacy of the welfare state per se. It built its electoral appeal on programs to make the welfare state more efficient, reduce cycles of dependency of citizens on government, and more broadly, increase the scope for entrepreneurial initiative by streamlining government regulation of business.

The second cleavage between the Left and Right emerged comparatively recently, in the 1970s and 1980s, and has had an oddly schizophrenic character.[5] At the time, it appeared to be a cleavage over "postmaterialist" values—self-realization, participatory politics, humanism, and environmentalism. By the 1990s, it was manifestly a division over "support for traditional moral and religious values, a strong defense, patriotism, law and order, opposition to immigration and minority rights, and respect for the traditional symbols and offices of authority."[6]

---

[3] See, for example, Kriesi et al. 2006, 2008; Kitschelt 1994, 1995; Inglehart 1977; van der Brug and van Spanje 2009.

[4] At various points in time, right-wing parties have challenged this. The founder of the Progress Party, the predecessor to the Danish People's Party, Morgens Glistrup, rose to prominence with his claim of paying no income tax, while the party program called for radical tax cuts and the virtual dismantling of government.

[5] For the seminal research on the "new politics" dimension, see Inglehart 1977, 1990.

[6] Cf. Flanagan 1987. The original research by Ronald Inglehart (1977) was based on a Maslowian conception of a needs hierarchy and suggested that the new dimension reflected progressive support for postmaterialistic self-realization. With materialistic needs fulfilled, the public could turn toward such issues. Yet as forcefully argued by Scott Flanagan (1987), there is not necessarily consensus among the postmaterialistically inclined about which specific cultural values to promote. In fact, just as one can observe a left and right on the materialistic or economic dimension, one can observe a left and right position on the new postmaterialistic issues. Some emphasize personal freedom and

Consistent with recent research, we call this second cleavage between the Left and Right the libertarian-authoritarian dimension.[7]

In the standard model, these two dimensions, economic redistribution and libertarian-authoritarian, define the ideological structure of western European politics. But we do not mean to suggest universal agreement. On the contrary, it is worth raising some large warning flags. Conceptually, the interpretation of the two ideological dimensions, and in particular the libertarian-authoritarian dimension, has provoked sharp debate.[8] Operationally, measures of the same ideological dimension vary from country to country, and even in the same country over time. Between these conceptual disputes, on the one hand, and differences in measurement, on the other, the distinction between the two dimensions across studies is clearer in some studies, and less so in others.[9] Yet having vigorously waved these warning flags, we find the picture of the ideological structure of contemporary party systems remarkably similar from country to country.[10]

Figure 4.1 presents a stylized representation of the ideological structure of the Danish party system, drawing on both surveys of public opinion and analyses of party manifestos. One dimension, shown on the horizontal axis, is economic redistribution: the farther to the left a party is on this dimension, the more socialist its program; the father to the right, the more liberal (in the European sense) is its program. The other dimension, depicted on the vertical axis, is the libertarian-authoritarian: the farther to the right a party is on this dimension, the stronger its commitment to cultural conservatism; the farther to the left, the stronger its commitment to cultural liberalism.

---

tolerance toward minorites. Others stress order, conformity to customs, and traditional values. In this way, the real fault line is not between cultural and economic values but rather over which cultural values should take prominence. This two-dimensional perspective has since been confirmed by other scholars such as Herbert Kitschelt (1994, 1995), Hanspeter Kriesi and his colleagues (2006, 2008), and Oddbjørn Knutsen and Staffan Kumlin (2005).

[7] For classic studies of the electoral emergence of the libertarian-authoritarian dimension in Denmark in the elections of 1990 and 1994, see Borre 1995; Borre and Andersen 1997. Cf. Stubager 2010.

[8] Inglehart 1987; Flanagan 1987.

[9] See Kriesi et al. 2006.

[10] Strikingly, this is true across measurement modes, especially surveys of public opinion and the analysis of party manifestos. It is worth remarking that the standard two-dimensional model includes the United States—a point of similarity that has escaped the attention it merits. See Jost, Frederico, and Napier 2009; Treier and Hillygus 2009.

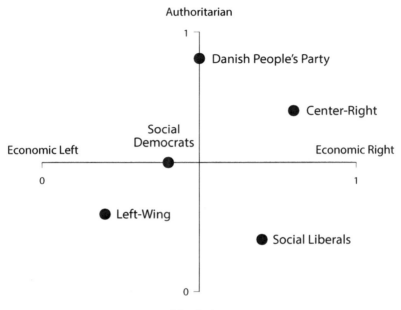

FIGURE 4.1 Illustration of the Two-dimensional Structure of the Danish
Party System

Note: This is an idealized graphic representation of the parties' position in the
two-dimensional ideological space based on analyses of party manifestos and the
positions of the voters of the respective parties.

The defining feature of this ideological structure is the independence
of the two left-right dimensions. As figure 4.1 shows, the economic redistribution and libertarian-authoritarian agendas are orthogonal. Economic egalitarianism and cultural conservatism are uncorrelated in the
electorate as a whole: knowing that a person is on the left (or right) on
one dimension is of little help in predicting whether they are on the left
(or right) on the other.[11]

More exactly, the two dimensions are orthogonal in *the electorate
taken as a whole*. Political parties win adherents precisely by embody-
ing distinctive combinations of positions on the two dimensions. Thus,
the left-wing parties are on the left on both dimensions, the center-right

[11] In the case of our study, the correlation between the measures of the two dimensions is zero.

parties are on the right on both dimensions, and the centrist Social Democrats are, to a first approximation, in the middle on each dimension. Two parties, however, combine contrasting positions on the two dimensions of left-right ideology. The Social Liberal Party is on the right on the economic redistribution dimension, but on the left on the libertarian-authoritarian dimension; the Danish People's Party tends to be on the left on the economic redistribution dimension on some strategic planks in particular—social assistance for the elderly, for example—but on the far right on the libertarian-authoritarian dimension.

This is the ideological space in which political parties compete for votes. Understandably in light of the rise of anti-immigration parties, research has focused on one of the "off diagonals": the combination of right-wing cultural conservatism and left-wing economic redistribution. A two-part argument has been advanced. First, it is ideologically self-contradictory to be on the Left when it comes to issues of economic redistribution, but on the Right when it comes to issues of cultural values.[12] Second, this contradictory combination of left and right values is at the heart of many anti-immigration parties, including, as figure 4.1 shows, the Danish People's Party. In analyzing this "contradictory" combination of ideological outlooks, research has aimed at identifying what distinguishes adherents of anti-immigration parties from supporters of mainstream parties. This research literature is vast, and continues to grow rapidly. Accordingly, we have chosen as our goal not to provide yet another analysis of adherents of these parties but to concentrate instead on those who still give their support to mainstream parties even though they hold the combination of values—economic egalitarianism and cultural conservatism—that render them susceptible to the appeal of anti-immigration parties.

Ideology and Anti-immigration Politics: Three Models

To map the structure of the party system, we have developed measures of the two primary ideological dimensions—economic redistribution and libertarian-authoritarian.[13] As far as possible, we have followed the

---

[12] Houtman, Achterberg, and Derks 2008. See also Elchardus and Spruyt 2012.
[13] Responses to the following items were used for the scale of respondents' positions on the libertarian-authoritarian dimension: "Violent crimes ought to be punished much harder than is currently the case"; "Economic growth should be ensured by expanding

examples of previous studies in constructing measures of the economic redistribution and libertarian-authoritarian dimensions.[14] To convey the flavor of the measure, here are two illustrations. An indicator of an authoritarian outlook is agreement with the statement that "violent crimes ought to be punished much harder than is currently the case." An indicator of a left-wing position on the economic redistribution dimension is the view that "high incomes should be taxed more than is currently the case." All measures are quite similar but not necessarily identical to measures in previous studies. It may be thought that the points of difference present a problem, yet it is just the other way around. Insofar as different measures of the same constructs yield the same results, a higher than ordinary degree of confidence in our findings is warranted.

The standard model of ideology provides a well-grounded explanatory platform for the analysis of electoral politics in general and anti-immigration politics in particular. According to the standard model, the two ideological dimensions structuring contemporary politics—economic redistribution and libertarian-authoritarian—are independent of one another.[15] Which ideological dimension is bound up with anti-immigration politics?

The question answers itself, apparently. The farther to the right that voters are on the libertarian-authoritarian dimension, the more importance they are likely to place on tradition, conformity, and obedience

---

industry, even if this is at the cost of environmental interests"; "As part of the War on Terror, the Danish Security and Intelligence Service should have far greater opportunities to gather information about all of us"; and "It would be very reasonable to let a strong man take over in an economic crisis." For economic redistribution, the items were: "The state has too little control over the business world"; "High incomes should be taxed more than is currently the case"; "In politics, one should strive to assure the same economic conditions for everyone, regardless of education and employment"; and "I am worried that the welfare state, as we know it today, is currently under threat." Items and the final variables are coded such that a high value reflects a right-wing position. On measures for further information, see appendix D.

[14] As in these previous studies, we assess respondents' positions on the ideological dimensions using questions about respondents' positions on specific policies related to each of the dimensions. For a thorough discussion, see Stubager 2006, 57–65. See also Borre 1995; Borre and Andersen 1997; Stubager 2010.

[15] As noted, the correlation between the two dimensions in our study is zero. But odd as it may sound, orthogonality, unlike pregnancy, is a matter of degree. Some studies have found a relationship between the two dimensions recovered by factor analysis (e.g., Kitschelt 1995). The relevant point is that the extent of the relationship is modest.

to established authority; the more circumscribed the range of their intellectual and aesthetic experience is likely to be; and as one consequence, the more rigid and stereotypical their thinking is likely to be.[16] Moreover, the farther to the right that voters are on the libertarian-authoritarian dimension, the more likely many of their sentiments about politics will be charged with hostility and contempt.[17] These two lines of argument—one cognitive and the other affective—are complementary, not competitive. The inference to draw from both is as plain as the nose on your face. The more authoritarian voters are in their political values, the more hostile to immigration and immigrants they are likely to be.

Granting this, a corollary follows from the geometry of two-dimensional structures. To say that the two dimensions of left-right are orthogonal is to assert that they are unrelated to one another. If the two dimensions are indeed independent of one another, then the centrality of the libertarian-authoritarian implies the irrelevance of the economic redistribution one. This reasoning has the support of over a decade of research across western Europe. Antipathy to immigrants, it has been repeatedly shown, is tied up with positions on the libertarian-authoritarian dimension and scarcely, if at all, attached to positions on the economic redistribution dimension.[18] Accordingly, we call this the established model of the ideological bases of anti-immigration politics.

The model is formally summarized in equation 4.1,

$$AI = a + b_1A + b_2E + u \qquad \text{(Eq. 4.1)}$$

where AI represents anti-immigrant sentiments, A is the location on the libertarian-authoritarian dimension, E is the location on the economic redistribution dimension, a is a constant, b_1 and b_2 are coefficients related to A and E, respectively, and u is an error term. In the established model, b_2 is presumed equal to zero.

It is our claim that the one-dimensional model is incomplete. The combination of cultural conservatism and economic egalitarianism produces

---

[16] We have in mind the construct of authoritarian aggression. For a remarkable research program providing evidentiary support for some of the most penetrating insights of the Frankfurt school's *The Authoritarian Personality*, see Altemeyer 1988.

[17] Altemeyer 1988.

[18] Borre 1995; Kitschelt 1995; Norris 2005; Stubager 2006.

a combustible reaction, we contend, thereby raising the level of hostility to immigrants above and beyond that attributable to right-wing authoritarian values on their own. We call this the combustibility hypothesis.

The combustibility hypothesis is formally expressed in equation 4.2,

$$AI = a + b_1A + b_2E + b_3E^*A + u \qquad \text{(Eq. 4.2)}$$

where the terms $b_1A + b_2E$ reflect the main effects of the libertarian-authoritarian and economic redistribution dimensions, and b_3E^*A their interaction.

Our argument implies three theoretical constraints on equation 4.2. The first constraint, $b_3 < 0$, signifies that the farther *to the right* citizens are on the libertarian-authoritarian dimension and *the farther to the left* they are on the economic redistribution dimension, the more negative their attitudes toward immigrants. The second constraint, $b_2 = 0$, indicates that beliefs about economic redistribution, in and of themselves, have no connection to attitudes toward immigrants. Thus, only when paired with a right-wing position on the libertarian-authoritarian dimension does an individual's position on economic redistribution become significantly related to that individual's anti-immigrant sentiments. The third constraint, $|b_1| > |b_3|$, signifies that notwithstanding the combustible interaction between the two dimensions, the primary driver of anti-immigrant attitudes is the libertarian-authoritarian dimension. These final constraints are meant to make it unmistakable that our aim is to add to previous research, not to reject it.

Our analysis proceeds in two steps. The first is to put our data and measures to the test by estimating the established model. This may sound like the wrong way around. It would fit standard protocol better to say that we were using our data and measures to test our new model. But it is important to show that when we analyze our data as others have theirs, we see just what they have seen. Accordingly, the first column of table 4.1 (i.e., model 1) reports the results of a regression of our attitudes toward immigrants scale on our measures of the libertarian-authoritarian and economic redistribution dimensions.[19]

---

[19] The attitudes toward immigrants scale consists of four items: "Immigrants must be able to preach and practice their religion in Denmark freely"; "Immigrants who have committed acts leading to prison sentences should be deported immediately"; "Foreigners should only be able to receive Danish citizenship after they have learned to act like

TABLE 4.1 A Test of the Combustibility Hypothesis (Excluding Danish People's Party Adherents): Effects of Libertarian-Authoritarian and Economic Redistribution Positions on Anti-immigrant Sentiments

	Model 1	Model 2
Intercept	0.16***	0.08***
	(0.01)	(0.02)
Libertarian-authoritarian position	0.57***	0.71***
	(0.02)	(0.04)
Economic redistribution position	−0.10***	0.04
	(0.02)	(0.04)
Libertarian-authoritarian × economic redistribution	—	−0.26***
		(0.06)
R^2	0.27	0.28

Note: N = 3,929. *** $p < 0.001$, ** $p < 0.01$, * $p < 0.05$. Entries are unstandardized OLS regression coefficients with standard errors in parentheses. The dependent variable, anti-immigrant sentiments, is coded to vary between 0 and 1, with high values reflecting high levels of anti-immigrant sentiments. Libertarian-authoritarian and economic redistribution positions are coded to vary between 0 and 1. On both variables, high values reflect more right-wing positions. We test our hypothesis among adherents of the political mainstream, and hence, exclude adherents of the Danish People's Party. All question wordings appear in appendix D.

The results in the first column line up squarely with the established model of anti-immigration politics. Right-wing authoritarian values are a strikingly strong predictor of antipathy to immigrants. A one-unit increase on the libertarian-authoritarian dimension translates into a six-tenths of a unit increase on the attitudes toward immigrants scale. Left-wing values on economic redistribution, it could be argued, also are tied up with antipathy to immigrants. A closer examination of the results, however, makes it plain that the relationship between the two, though statistically significant, is substantively trivial.

Our results therefore parallel those of previous research. The distinctive prediction of the combustibility hypothesis is that the combination of economic egalitarianism and cultural conservatism boosts anti-immigrant sentiments above and beyond the independent effects

---

a Dane"; and "If there are not enough jobs, employers should employ Danes ahead of immigrants." Items and the final variable are coded such that a high value reflects a high level of anti-immigrant sentiment; see appendix D.

of either or both. The test of the combustibility hypothesis, it follows, is the interaction term b_3. If this term is not substantively significant, the hypothesis fails.

The results in the second column of table 4.1 are telling on two counts. The more consequential is that the interaction term manifestly is significant, not merely statistically, but also substantively. It is important to emphasize that right-wing authoritarian values are still the strongest predictor of anti-immigrant attitudes. But the combustible effect of combining economic egalitarianism with cultural conservatism is consequential: for a one-unit change in the interaction term, there is a one-quarter of a unit increase in anti-immigrant sentiments. This conforms nicely with the first and third theoretical constraints in equation 4.2.

This test of the combustibility hypothesis is reassuring in another respect. The results in the first column of table 4.1 give the impression that economic egalitarianism contributes to anti-immigrant sentiments—modestly to be sure, but noticeable all the same. The test of the full model, though, shows that this impression is misleading. Favoring economic redistribution is not in and of itself associated with anti-immigrant sentiments. It is connected with such feelings only when it is combined with being on the right on the libertarian-authoritarian dimension, which conforms to the second theoretical constraint in equation 4.2.

What is the political significance of these findings? As we would like to underscore, they do *not* speak to why voters become adherents of anti-immigration parties. Supporters of the Danish People's Party were excluded from the analysis. The political significance lies in just the opposite direction. The discovery of an interaction between cultural conservatism and economic egalitariansim brings to light a constituency in the electorate that does not yet support an anti-immigration party but has an ideological cast of mind that opens it to an appeal by such a party. It is not foreordained that this constituency will support a party like the Danish People's Party. Issues other than immigration may dominate its thinking. But it is ripe for mobilization. The interaction of economic egalitarianism and cultural conservatism points to a potential flash point in contemporary politics.

Replication of the Flash Point Conjecture

The flash point conjecture, if valid, demonstrates that there is a constituency in the electorate that can propel the Danish People's Party to the forefront. But before venturing an explanation of what we have found, we think it is vital to show that ours is not merely a chance result. Obstacles litter our route to replication, however. No other study has measures that exactly duplicate our measures. As seriously, the measures in other studies are shorter and therefore less reliable than ours.[20] We nonetheless will now bring to bear every study with even approximately comparable measures, reanalyzing them to determine if their results are consistent with ours or kick the props out from under them. It is perfectly possible—indeed, a prudent person would say that it is quite likely—that the results from other studies will differ from ours, even if the flash point claim is valid. This is a risk. All the same, we count these differences in measurement as an asset, not a liability. Insofar as the results of other studies are consistent with the combustibility hypothesis *notwithstanding all the points of difference in measurement,* the evidence supporting the flash point conjecture is stronger, not weaker.

In all, only four studies give us any chance to replicate our analysis: the Danish National Election Studies of 2007, 2005, 2001, and 1998. The points of difference between the measure of left-wing economic values and right-wing social values in the Cartoon Crisis study along with the measures in the replication studies include the number of items (four in ours versus two in the others), direction of wording (one reversal in ours versus none in the others), and response format (five in ours versus four in the others). Given that these studies used different measures from ours and were conducted at different points in time from ours, an attempt at replication may seem foolhardy. Still, we felt strongly the importance of testing the robustness of the ideological interaction finding from our study. So we decided to let the chips fall where they may.

---

[20] For further information, see the online appendix (http://press.princeton.edu/titles/10400.html).

TABLE 4.2 Replication Tests of the Combustibility Hypothesis: Danish
National Election Studies, 1998–2007

	1998	2001	2005	2007
Intercept	−0.08	−0.10*	−0.02	−0.01
	(0.04)	(0.05)	(0.04)	(0.03)
Libertarian-authoritarian	1.03***	1.02***	0.90***	0.95***
position	(0.06)	(0.07)	(0.06)	(0.05)
Economic redistribution	0.08	0.20*	−0.06	−0.04
position	(0.07)	(0.08)	(0.07)	(0.06)
Libertarian-authoritarian ×	−0.22*	−0.39**	−0.19†	−0.31**
economic redistribution	(0.11)	(0.12)	(0.11)	(0.10)
R^2	0.41	0.35	0.36	0.39
N	1,394	1,390	1,555	2,275

Note: *** $p < 0.001$, ** $p < 0.01$, * $p < 0.05$, † $p < 0.10$. Entries are unstandardized
OLS regression coefficients with standard errors in parentheses. The dependent variable,
anti-immigrant sentiments, is coded to vary between 0 and 1 with high values reflecting
high levels of anti-immigrant sentiments. Libertarian-authoritarian and economic redistribution positions are coded to vary between 0 and 1. On both variables, high values
reflect more right-wing positions. We test our hypothesis among adherents of the political mainstream, and hence, exclude adherents of the Danish People's Party. All question
wordings appear in the online appendix (http://press.princeton.edu/titles/10400.html).
Data are from the Danish National Election Study in the given years.

For all four studies, we estimated the combustibility model summarized in equation 4.2. The results are shown in table 4.2. The key question is whether the interaction term, b_3, is significant and appropriately
signed (i.e., negative). The answer for the 2007 study is yes; it is also
yes for the 2001 study, and yet again yes for the 1998 study. The one exception is the 2005 study. There the interaction coefficient fails to meet
the conventional standard of statistical significance. It is significant at
$p = 0.086$ in a two-tailed test as opposed to the ritual threshold of 0.05.
The 0.05 level is a mere convention. We count this result as a failure to
replicate because others might do so, and not because we do.[21]

We have put all our cards on the table. Notwithstanding differences
in measurement and points in time, four times out of five the interaction term is significant. Those who are cultural conservatives *and*

---

[21] It should also be noted that the substantive difference between the significant coefficient in 1998 (0.22) and the insignificant one in 2005 (0.19) is trivial.

economic egalitarians are even more hostile to immigrants than those who are just cultural conservatives. This combination of left-wing economic values and right-wing social values cries out for analysis. We call voters who view politics through this lens the traditionalist Left—traditionalist, because they cleave to cultural conservatism; and Left, because they cleave to social and economic egalitarianism.

AN OBVIOUS STARTING POINT AND A PUZZLE

Why is the effect of combining left-wing economic values and right-wing social values combustible? An explanatory starting point is obvious: the cultural conservatism of the traditionalist Left. Such leftists have a defensive attachment to traditional values, one can readily imagine, because they perceive immigrants to be a threat to the cultural identity of their country. "They"—that is, immigrants—have different values. "They" don't fit in, and what is more, "they" don't want to fit in. "They" actively resist identifying with or adopting Danish values and traditions. Or so it seems to the traditionalists. If this last belief is what is evoking an especially strong anti-immigrant reaction from the traditionalist Left, they will be especially likely to perceive a threat to the Danish way of life. Figure 4.2 presents a test of this reasoning. It displays levels of perceptions of a threat to cultural identity as a function of how far to the left or right people are on the two primary ideological dimensions—authoritarian-libertarian and economic redistribution. The higher the score, the higher the level of (perceived) threat to the Danish culture and way of life. In deference to convention, we will refer to those in the lower left-hand corner of figure 4.2 as the ideological Left, since they are consistently on the left on both dimensions, and those who fall in the upper right-hand cell as the ideological Right, since they are consistently on the right on both dimensions.

Informed commentary, not to mention some scholarship, would lead one to suppose that the popular antipathy toward immigrants is being driven by a clash of ways of life. Yet the first feature of figure 4.2 that stands out is the minimal level of perceptions of threat to Danish culture throughout the largest part of the electorate. Consider the ideological Right in the upper-right corner of figure 4.2—that is, those who are conservative on both ideological dimensions. Like the dog in

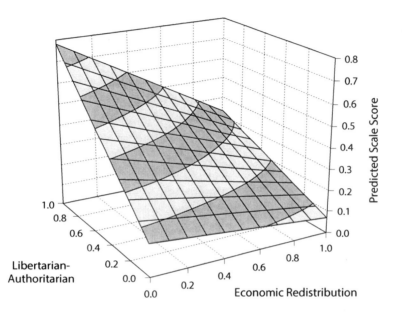

FIGURE 4.2. Effects of Positions on the Libertarian-Authoritarian and Economic Redistribution Dimensions for "Perceived Cultural Threat" (Predicted Scores)

Note: N = 1548. The figure displays the predicted scores for cultural threat as a function of position on the libertarian-authoritarian and economic redistribution dimensions, and their interaction. The regression equation from which predicted scores are calculated is: cultural threat = 0.15*** + 0.63*** × A − 0.08 × E − 0.37** × A × E, where A is positioned on the libertarian-authoritarian dimension, E is positioned on the economic redistribution dimension, and stars indicate significance: *** $p < 0.001$, ** $p < 0.01$, * $p < 0.05$. We test our hypothesis among adherents of the political mainstream, and hence, exclude adherents of the Danish People's Party. The question wording for the dependent variable, cultural threat, is: "I am afraid that Danish culture is presently under threat." The response categories were: completely agree, somewhat agree, neither/nor, somewhat disagree, completely disagree, or don't know. The respondents who answered "don't know" are excluded from the analyses. The answers were recoded to vary between 0 and 1, and reversed such that a high value indicates high levels of perceived threat. On both ideology variables, high values reflect right-wing positions.

the Sherlock Holmes story that provided the tip-off clue by not barking at an "intruder," it is what is not the case that is instructive. The ideological Right is *not* up in arms about a threat to cultural identity. It is true that levels of perceived threat are higher among the ideological Right than among the ideological Left in the lower-left corner. But it is the modesty of the differences between the two, not the mere fact that they differ, that is striking.

The second feature in figure 4.2 that leaps out is the spike in the level of perceived threat as graphed in the top left-hand corner. The traditionalist Left tends to perceive a threat to its country's way of life. It is not even that these leftists are more likely to do so than the ideological Right. It is that they are so much more likely—indeed, one is tempted to say, uniquely likely—to perceive a threat to the Danish culture. Their score is higher by a factor of three than that of the ideological Left. This represents a deep cleavage between the Right and Left, albeit not a surprising one. What is startling is the cleavage on the right. The level of perceived threat to cultural identity among the traditionalist Left is nearly twice as high as among the ideological Right.

This result may seem like the final nail in the coffin. The diagnostic feature of the traditionalist Left is its perception of a threat to the national culture and identity. But the root of these feelings goes deeper, we believe. Yes, these leftists express their feelings of vulnerability by calling up a threat in their minds that Muslims pose to the established culture of their country. But we suspect that they would feel the same even in the absence of Muslim immigrants.

Creating a counterfactual world in which there are no Muslim immigrants is not within anyone's power. It is within our power, though, to investigate more deeply the clash of ways of life hypothesis. If the cultural clash generated by Muslim immigrants is setting off the explosive reaction of the traditionalist Left against immigrants, then the traditionalist Left should be distinctively likely to dislike Muslims. It should also be distinctly ready to perceive them as a threat.

Figures 4.3 and 4.4 present the results of this pair of tests concerning the clash of ways of life hypothesis. Figure 4.3 reports predicted levels (on a scale of 0 to 1) of levels of dislike of Muslims as a product simultaneously of respondents' positions on the two ideological dimensions that organize Danish politics—libertarian-authoritarian and economic redistribution. It is of course the distinctiveness—or lack thereof—of the group in the upper left-hand corner, the traditionalist Left, that is pivotal.

As we have just seen, the traditionalist Left stands out by its degree of fear that the Danish culture is threatened. But it does not stand out

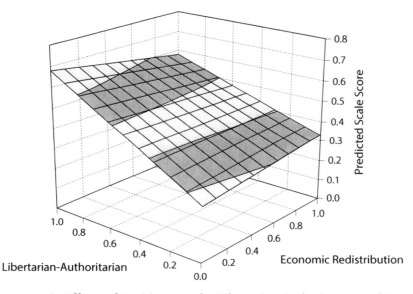

FIGURE 4.3. Effects of Positions on the Libertarian-Authoritarian and Economic Redistribution Dimensions for "Dislike for Muslims" (Predicted Scores)

Note: N = 1,494. The figure displays the predicted scores for dislike for Muslims as a function of position on the libertarian-authoritarian and economic redistribution dimensions, and their interaction. The regression equation from which predicted scores are calculated is: cultural threat = $0.26^{***} + 0.42^{***} \times A + 0.07 \times E - 0.18 \times A \times E$, where A is positioned on the libertarian-authoritarian dimension, E is positioned on the economic redistribution dimension, and stars indicate significance: $^{***} p < 0.001$, $^{**} p < 0.01$, $^{*} p < 0.05$. We test our hypothesis among adherents of the political mainstream, and hence, exclude adherents of the Danish People's Party. The question wording for the dependent variable, dislike for Muslims, is: "What about Muslims—how much do you like them?" The responses were obtained on 0–10 scales with the end points labeled "Do not like the group at all" (0) and "Like the group very much" (10). The respondents who answered "don't know" are excluded from the analyses. The answers were recoded to vary between 0 and 1, and reversed such that a high value indicates high levels of dislike. On both ideology variables, high values reflect right-wing positions.

by its degree of dislike for Muslims. True, these leftists' scores are significantly higher than the scores of those who are consistently to the left on both dimensions. Yet so, too, are the scores of the ideological Right. And strikingly, the scores of the traditionalist Left are roughly similar to those of the ideological Right. Figure 4.4 presents a second test of this line of reasoning, this time focusing on the degree to which

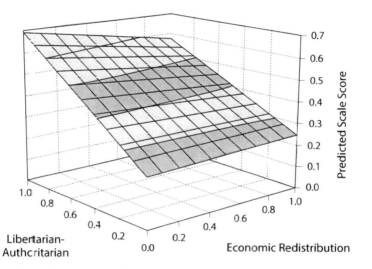

FIGURE 4.4. Effects of Positions on the Libertarian-Authoritarian and Economic Redistribution Dimensions for "Perceived Threat from Muslims" (Predicted Scores)

Note: N = 1,534. The figure displays the predicted scores for perceived threat from Muslims as a function of position on the libertarian-authoritarian and economic redistribution dimensions, and their interaction. The regression equation from which predicted scores are calculated is: perceived threat from Muslims = 0. 22*** + 0.47*** × A + 0.02 × E − 0.14 × A × E, where A is positioned on the libertarian-authoritarian dimension, E is positioned on the economic redistribution dimension, and stars indicate significance: *** p < 0.001, ** p < 0.01, * p < 0.05. We test our hypothesis among adherents of the political mainstream, and hence, exclude adherents of the Danish People's Party. The question wording for the dependent variable, perceived threat from Muslims, is: "What about Muslims—how threatening do you feel they are?" The responses were obtained on 0–10 scales with the end points labeled "The group does not pose any threat" (0) and "The group poses a great threat" (10). The respondents who answered "don't know" are excluded from the analyses. The variable was recoded to vary between 0 and 1 with a high value indicating a high level of perceived threat from Muslims. On both ideology variables, high values reflect right-wing positions.

the traditionalist Left perceives Muslims to be a threat. The results are the same. Again, the traditionalist Left and ideological Right are fairly similar.[22]

---

[22] Another way to put these results is to note that b_3, the coefficient of the interaction between the authoritarian-libertarian and economic redistribution dimensions in the model, is insignificant in the models that lie behind figures 4.3 and 4.4.

This set of results thus presents a puzzle. The traditionalist Left stands apart from everyone else, including the ideological Right, in its concern that immigration poses a serious threat to the Danish national character. But the traditionalist Left and ideological Right do not significantly differ in the degree to which they dislike Muslims or feel threatened by them. This suggests, we believe, that their readiness to see threats to the national character may go beyond concern with an extrinsic factor like immigration.

COMMUNITARIANISM AS AN IDEOLOGY

The traditionalist Left, as mentioned above, is distinguished by a political outlook blending left-wing values on economic issues and right-wing ones on cultural values. To many political analysts, this combination of social egalitarianism and cultural conservatism is self-contradictory, or even, in the view of some, "unnatural."[23] So it may appear to a political theorist. But there is much difference between the perspectives of a theorist and a citizen. As Aristotle famously responded to Plato, the person wearing the shoes, not the cobbler who has made them, decides whether they fit or not. So we began with a conversation with John, relying on his concerns, expressed in his words, to bring our ideas to life. Now it is time to express these ideas directly, explicitly.

Starting Point

The analysis of the politics of immigrants and social welfare in chapter 3 rested on the premise that there is a social covenant. The right to claim support from the welfare state is based on the duty to contribute to it. It is our hypothesis that for many, this egalitarian covenant is part of a conception of communitarianism built on a tradition of social values and rules defining the obligations of each member of the community to the other members. How should one behave in public? Who is owed respect? How important is it to live by community standards?

Two generations ago—even one generation ago—there was a widely shared understanding that a properly lived life encompasses, among

---

[23] Houtman, Achterberg, and Derks 2008.

other things, the role of religious faith in giving meaning and guidance to everyday life, the grounding of family in the bonds of marriage, and the importance of respect for one's elders, self-restraint, and order in the larger community. To be sure, the traditional culture of Denmark was more liberal and open-minded than that of a country like the Netherlands.[24] Even so, and even as late as the mid-twentieth century, the larger culture of Denmark bore the mark of "Lutheran farmers and the provincial middle class," with their commitment to the values of discipline, tradition, and piety.[25] The culture was especially marked by a commitment to the importance of membership in a common community rather than the self-realization of each person as a unique individual.

It should be unnecessary to add, but in a litigious era it is all the same prudent to do so, that we are far from claiming that Danish culture prior to the 1970s was monolithic. There were many strands, including some committed to innovation and experimentation, particularly in the arts.[26] Ours is a limited claim. It is that the combination of social egalitarianism and cultural conservatism represented—and represents—a common outlook in Danish society. It is deeply ahistorical to characterize this combination of values as unnatural. On the contrary, it is a part of the woof and warp of Danish culture.[27] What is more, a traditionalist Left outlook on life and society, though not as dominant as fifty years ago, remains an integral component of the Danish electorate. Public opinion studies from the last decade of the twentieth century and the largest part of the first decade of the twenty-first century suggest that the traditionalist Left has decreased.[28] Yet if it is no longer the most common outlook on life and politics, it remains an exceedingly typical one, held by roughly one out of every three Danes.

[24] Jespersen 2004. See especially the discussion of the teaching of N.F.S. Grundtvig, with its commitment to the idea that individuals are humans before they are Christians.

[25] Klausen 2009.

[26] An especially prominent example in the 1930s was Poul Henningsen.

[27] In saying that the combination of social egalitarianism and cultural conservatism is distinctively Danish, we were not at all asserting that it is peculiarly or uniquely Danish.

[28] Borre 2007, 183. It should be noted that some of the items underlying the measure of ideology are sensitive to changes in policy (e.g., "Violent crime should be punished harder than is currently the case"). In this way, some of the changes in ideological positions could reflect contextual changes rather than actual shifting ideological positions.

What is the world like in which the traditionalist Left now lives? Transformative changes in the economy, society, and culture have pushed it to the margins of society—the premise of our theory. In this theory, the concept of beliefs and marginalization do equal work. The traditionalist Left holds to a coherent view of life and society. And it is because the traditionalist Left genuinely believes in this view of life and society that the cultural, economic, and social changes over the last generation have left these adherents feeling marginalized in their own society.

Marginalized in what ways? As a normative ideal, and to an impressive degree as an empirical fact, their Denmark "could be described as a gigantic village, where uniformity predominated and social distances were modest," where families had lived for generations, and everyone knew and was known by everyone else.[29] Over the last long generation, though, there has been a deep tidal wave of change. Compared to today, the culture of the past was conservative, religious, restrictive, and conformist. Compared to the past, the culture of today is liberal, secular, provocative, and individualist. In the wake of this transformation in the core culture, profound changes have occurred in core social institutions and accepted practice, including shifts in the presumption of marriage as a basis for partnership along with an acceptance, and even an institutionalization, of alternative lifestyles and sexual orientations. As Jytte Klausen (2009, 61) has noted, "The tolerance, openness, and secular values that a number of Western European countries now claim as essential national values are in fact recent inventions, born during the anticlerical social liberation movements of the 1970s."

The undertow of all these changes has dragged those with a traditional, conservative outlook on life from the place that they held in the society they grew up in to one at the margins of the society they now live in. To a degree unimaginable only a half century ago, immigration and the issues it has brought to the fore have further aggravated the traditionalist Left's feeling of marginalization. Once a famously homogeneous culture, Denmark has become heterogeneous. Immigration (even with recent restrictions) outstrips emigration, and for the last three decades (particularly before the tightening of regulations in

---

[29] Jespersen 2004, 111.

2002), immigrants—most of them Muslim—have predominantly come from eastern Europe and Turkey. Compared to other countries in western Europe, the relative proportion of immigrants is not large.[30] But partly because of the concentration of immigrants in specific housing areas, and partly because of the public visibility of differences in dress, religious practices, language, and (especially for women) demeanor, the fact of difference has become an everyday feature of public life in (urban) Denmark. The result is to challenge the traditionalist Left's conception of community on many sides—the loss of cultural homogeneity; the burdens that the new immigrants are placing on public resources and, even more so, their apparent lack of commitment to the moral covenant underpinning the welfare state; the transformation of a primarily rural economy into a high human capital economy; the loss of a village culture where everyone knew and was known by everyone else to the impersonal, disruptive lifestyles of cities; and the conversion of Denmark from a religious society to the very model of a secular society along with the assaultive challenges to traditions that come with this conversion.

What is at stake for the traditionalist Left, in its view of the world, is a vision of communitarianism that combines a commitment to both social egalitarianism and cultural conservatism. And as we are suggesting, those who hold to this two-pronged vision of the ideal society feel marginalized by both changes *within* Danish society and shocks from *without.* From the perspective of those who no longer feel at the center of Danish society, change in Danish values and its sense of itself as a community threaten its national character. These shifts are immanent in Danish society, thus threatening the traditional identity of Danish society, quite apart from immigrants and their impact.

The relationships between a sense of marginalization and ideological commitments are deeply ambiguous. A particular vision of community is being challenged, but is it one of community as it was then or as it is remembered now? Modesty is called for on the part of analysts. The fact of change is real. The absence of direct evidence is no less real.

---

[30] In January 2006, according to Statistics Denmark, around 7.5 percent of the Danish population was born outside Denmark. According to Lene Kühle (2006), there were around two hundred thousand Muslims living in Denmark as of January 1, 2006, corresponding to 3.7 percent of the total population.

Still, skepticism about an ideal (idealized?) past has proven its worth before in the analysis of collective memory. And if there is not direct evidence at hand, indirect evidence can be brought to bear.

What should be the case if those who feel that the cohesion of society as it was when they were young has been lost? The processes of secularization and liberalization are not instantaneous. They unfold over time. For any given individual, the degree or intensity of change should be proportional to their age. The older a person is, the greater the difference in the dominant ethos at the point that they were being socialized and the moment, now, that they are attempting to recall the ethos of society when they were young. Concretely, older people grew up in a more homogeneous, communitarian Denmark than younger people. If it is the loss of a past that was real rather than idealized that is fueling the specially sharp degree of resentment and anger at immigrants, then the combination of right-wing social values and left-wing economic ones is especially combustible for older respondents. In fact, the interaction between authoritarian values and economic egalitarianism reported in table 4.1 is significant for all age groups. This implies that the heightened hostility toward immigrants among the traditionalist Left is not contingent on having in fact experienced the actual changes in society over the last long generation. The loss of community, this suggests, is the loss of an imagined, not a remembered, community.[31]

Diagnostics of Marginalization

As a result of transformative changes in the Danish economy and society, a more secular, affluent, materialist society has emerged at the expense of an older, traditionalist, communitarian culture. In the mind of a traditionalist, this new society is marked by a loss of social solidarity intertwined with a rise of egoism. Egoists care only for their own welfare, not the community's. A world of egoists is one in which you must

---

[31] It could turn out that the sense of insecurity and threat is a driver of the individual's ideological outlook as opposed to vice versa (see, for example, Oxley et al. 2008). To the threatened individual, the combination of a large caretaking government and a culture constraining divergence is, psychologically speaking, attractive as a protective measure. In this view, individual differences in feelings of insecurity are chronic and social changes are not so much something that are causing these feelings as something merely blamed for them (i.e., used as targets for frustration).

always be on guard. It is not simply that you cannot count on them to be trustworthy, in the sense of relying on them to keep their word. It is that they represent a threat: they will take advantage of you if they can.

Our study includes two measures on this point. One is the idea that there are few people you can trust completely. Figure 4.5 shows reactions to a proposition related to the belief that others cannot be trusted, and how these reactions depend on people's outlooks on the two fundamental ideological dimensions—libertarian-authoritarian and economic redistribution.

As is seen in figure 4.5, the farther to the right respondents are on the libertarian-authoritarian dimension, the more likely they are to feel that "you cannot be too careful when dealing with others." There are no surprises here: this is what previous research has found.[32] But what previous research has not uncovered is the combustible effect of combining cultural conservatism and economic egalitarianism. Notwithstanding the fact that those with right-wing values on the libertarian-authoritarian dimension tend to lack trust in others in general, those who also have left-wing values on the economic redistribution dimension are even more likely to do so. As seen in the upper part of figure 4.5, the lack of trust is two times as high among the traditionalist Left as compared to the ideological Right.

Our other measure speaks to the loss of social solidarity because of the ascendancy of selfishness. It captures the feeling of having always to be on guard because people now are concerned only about what is good for them. Figure 4.6 summarizes reactions to the proposition "Other people will exploit you if you are not careful." Again, reactions are calculated as a function of people's outlooks on the two fundamental ideological dimensions—libertarian-authoritarian and economic redistribution. And again, notwithstanding the general tendency of those with right-wing cultural values to mistrust others, those who combine cultural conservatism with left-wing economic values are strikingly more likely to do so.

On our line of reasoning, the traditionalist Left feels marginalized. One indicator of this marginalization is the distance these leftists feel between the politics of their time and themselves. To illustrate this, let

[32] Duckitt 2001; Sibley. Wilson, and Duckitt 2007.

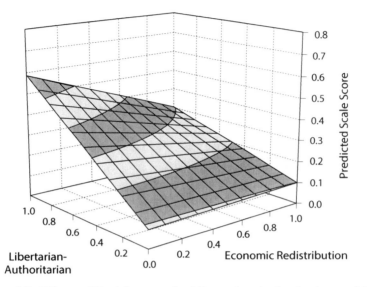

FIGURE 4.5. Effects of Positions on the Libertarian-Authoritarian and Economic Redistribution Dimensions on the Belief That One "Cannot Be Too Careful in Dealing with Other People" (Predicted Scores)

Note: N = 3,097. The figure displays the predicted scores for cannot be too careful as a function of position on the libertarian-authoritarian and economic redistribution dimensions, and their interaction. The regression equation from which predicted scores are calculated is: cannot be too careful = 0.08*** + 0.50*** × A + 0.02 × E − 0.30*** × A × E, where A is positioned on the libertarian-authoritarian dimension, E is positioned on the economic redistribution dimension, and stars indicate significance: *** p < 0.001, ** p < 0.01, * p < 0.05. We test our hypothesis among adherents of the political mainstream, and hence, exclude adherents of the Danish People's Party. The question wording for the dependent variable, cannot be too careful, is: "Do you think that you can trust most people, or do you think that you can't be too careful when dealing with others?" The response categories were: most people can be trusted, it depends, you cannot be too careful, and don't know. The respondents who answered "don't know" are excluded from the analyses. The variable was recoded to vary between 0 and 1 with a high value reflecting the belief that one cannot be too careful when dealing with others. On both ideology variables, high values reflect right-wing positions.

us return to John. Asked what he thinks about when the word politics is mentioned, John replies,

> Well, um, if I may say so, I've been very interested in politics, but well, now as I'm growing older, I'm not really interested anymore. I, and it's probably also because, you know, I'm getting older, and

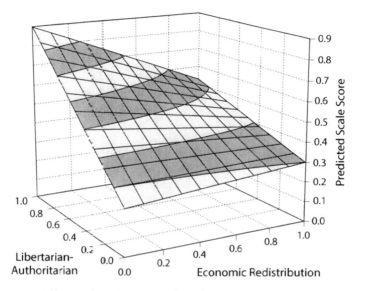

FIGURE 4.6. Effects of Positions on the Libertarian-Authoritarian and Economic Redistribution Dimensions on the Belief That "Other People Will Take Advantage of You" (Predicted Scores)

Note: N = 3,092. The figure displays the predicted scores for other people will take advantage as a function of position on the libertarian-authoritarian and economic redistribution dimensions, and their interaction. The regression equation from which predicted scores are calculated is: other people will take advantage = 0.23*** + 0.67*** × A + 0.07 × E − 0.44*** × A × E, where A is positioned on the libertarian-authoritarian dimension, E is positioned on the economic redistribution dimension, and stars indicate significance: *** $p < 0.001$, ** $p < 0.01$, * $p < 0.05$. We test our hypothesis among adherents of the political mainstream, and hence, exclude adherents of the Danish People's Party. The question wording for the dependent variable, other people will take advantage, is: "Other people will exploit you if you are not careful." The response categories were: completely agree, somewhat agree, neither/nor, somewhat disagree, completely disagree, and don't know. The respondents who answered "don't know" are excluded from the analyses. The variable was recoded to vary between 0 and 1 with a high value reflecting the belief that other people will take advantage of you. On both ideology variables, high values reflect right-wing positions.

then you get fed up with it. Before, when you were young, you could take it much better, you know, and say no, let's get on, now we're left behind, but we continue, don't we? Well, today, to put it straight, I don't fancy listening to any of them. And that goes for both the prime minister and right on to the other wing. In my opinion, they're more or less the same. I think, to put it in the language I usually use, and I've thought so for years, I think, to put it frankly that they're a bunch of loud nonsense talkers.[33]

John's answer is open to more than one interpretation, not because it is self-contradictory, we would emphasize, but because he is saying more than one thing. He was interested in politics when he was young, he explains. Now, in part, because "I'm getting older, and then you get fed up with it," there is, he implies, a natural life cycle effect—a disillusionment that comes with mere exposure to the chicanery of politicians. But there is more than a life cycle effect at work. His expression "now we're left behind" is telling. He goes on to note that "today, to put it straight, I don't fancy listening to any of them. And that goes for both the prime minister and right on to the other wing." Asked if he wants to hear about politics, he responds that the declarations of politicians are "filled with lies. They say one thing and do something else."

The effect of this across-the-board cynicism is all too predictable: distancing oneself from politics, including discussions of it. Asked whether he wants to hear about politics, John replies, "No, generally speaking no. Well, that is if there's some political debate on the telly, I might just take a look at it, but definitely no more than that. No more, well, I said some time in the past, not so long ago, said to myself, 'You don't take part in it anymore, you don't care anymore.'"

One diagnostic sign of political disengagement along with inattention and indifference to politics is a deficit of knowledge about it. In speaking of a deficit of political knowledge, we do not mean a lack of knowledge of the political history of one's country. Instead, what we have in mind is a lack of knowledge about its current affairs. Accordingly, we have built a scale of knowledge of current political facts, some obvious—such as which parties form the current government—and some less so—such as which level of government manages the hospitals in Denmark following the municipal reform.[34]

---

[33] The literal translation is foghorns (i.e., on a ship).

[34] We measured political knowledge by using six general political knowledge questions, summed to an index ($\alpha = 0.71$). The questions read: "Which parties are members of the current government?" (Liberals and Conservative); "Which party does Lotte Bundsgaard belong to?" (Social Democrats); "After the municipal reform, which level of government assumes responsibility for managing the hospitals in Denmark?" (regional); "Some of the political parties are more favorable than others toward refugees and immigrants. Are the Social Liberals more or less favorable toward refugees and immigrants?"

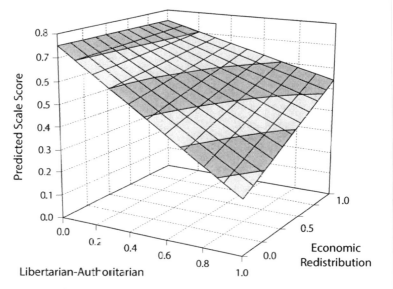

FIGURE 4.7. Effects cf Positions on the Libertarian-Authoritarian and Economic Redistribution Dimensions on "Political Knowledge" (Predicted Scores)

Note: N = 4,639. The figure displays the predicted scores for political knowledge as a function of position on the libertarian-authoritarian and economic redistribution dimensions, and their interaction. The regression equation from which predicted scores are calculated is: political knowledge = 0.75*** − 0.522*** × A − 0.01 × E + 0.32*** × A × E, where A is positioned on the libertarian-authoritarian dimension, E is positioned on the economic redistribution dimension, and stars indicate significance: *** $p < 0.001$, ** $p < 0.01$, * $p < 0.05$. We test our hypothesis among adherents of the political mainstream, and hence, exclude adherents of the Danish People's Party. Political knowledge is based on an index of questions. Political knowledge is coded to vary between 0 and 1 with a high value reflecting a high level of knowledge. On both ideology variables, high values reflect right-wing positions.

If our hypothesis about feelings of marginalization characterizing the traditionalist Left is broadly correct, these leftists should be set apart from the other respondents in our survey by a lack of knowledge about current affairs in politics. Figure 4.7 tests this prediction. Again, the combustibility hypothesis wins support. Those who are on the left on economic redistribution but on the right on the

---

(more favorable); "There are also some parties that place greater emphasis on tax cuts than others. Are the Conservatives among the parties that place more or less emphasis on immediate tax cuts?" (more emphasis); and "Which country is hosting the EU presidency this spring?" (Austria).

libertarian-authoritarian dimension score strikingly low on the scale of political knowledge (here placed in the lower-left corner). Still more important, although just as committed to cultural conservatism, the traditionalist Left is decisively different from the ideological Right and dramatically different from the ideological Left.

The traditionalist Left was at the center of the world that it grew up in—a world governed by a communitarian compact. And the heart of this compact, as John repeatedly remarked, was a "feeling of community," a sense that everyone was in it together with everyone else. It is this sense that has been lost, and with it the follow-on loss of security that comes from belonging to a community pledged to protect one's well-being. Now, if it is not a contradiction in terms, society is a society of egoists interested only in their own well-being.

A CONJECTURE ABOUT A POLITICAL FAULT LINE

The all-too-familiar phrase "we will show that the 'conventional wisdom' is wrong" has not appeared on a page up to this point and will not make a last-minute appearance now. Our objective has been to extend previous research, not to reject it. The focus of previous work has been the rise of radical Right parties—appropriately so, because the emergence of these parties is the most dramatic change in the party systems of western European politics in a generation, and represents a gathering threat to a liberal society. Given the volume of research on the radical Right, the question we asked ourselves was, How could we best add to the stock of knowledge about anti-immigration politics? The answer was by turning away from the political extremes and concentrating our attention instead on the political mainstream. Hence our decision to exclude adherents of the Danish People's Party from our analysis and zero in on supporters of mainline parties.

More particularly, our concern has been the ideological bases of anti-immigrant attitudes. Consistent with previous research, our analyses show that right-wing cultural values are far and away the dominant ideological force driving aversion to immigrants. But we also had an intuition that this was not the whole story. And the combination of right-wing cultural values and left-wing economic ones, as our reasoning anticipated and our results show, adds to the rejection of immigrants above and beyond right-wing cultural values.

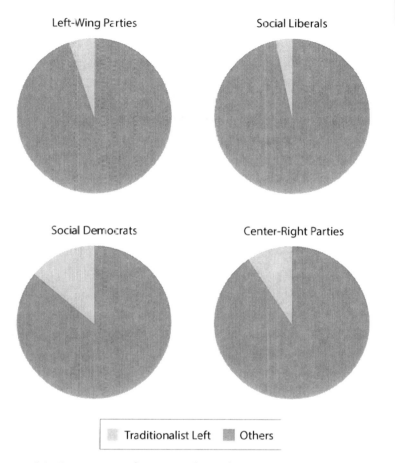

Left-Wing Parties   Social Liberals

Social Democrats   Center-Right Parties

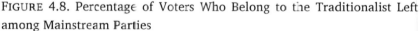

Traditionalist Left   Others

FIGURE 4.8. Percentage of Voters Who Belong to the Traditionalist Left among Mainstream Parties

Note: The figure is calculated from trichotomized versions of the libertarian-authoritarian and economic redistribution scales. Hence, the proportion of traditionalist Left is the proportion within each party that simultaneously is among the third-most right wing or cultural issues and the third-most left wing on economic issues.

Grant, then, that the combustibility hypothesis is correct—and we investigated every relevant study to replicate the results of our own. Where are the voters who are not yet adherents of the anti-immigration party but are ideologically susceptible to its appeal concentrated in the contemporary party system? Figure 4.8 shows the percentage within each of the mainstream "parties" of those who are on the left on the economic redistribution dimension and—also—on the right on the libertarian-authoritarian dimension.

These figures should be taken as only suggestive, since the cutoff defining who is on the left and right on the two dimensions of ideology are based on the standard—but arbitrary—rule of trichotomization. The two "parties" in which there is a relative combustible concentration are the center-right (i.e., the Liberal Party and Conservatives), and still more, the Social Democrats. The fault line, this indicates, runs down the middle of the political spectrum. It is there that the ideological fuel propelling anti-immigration politics has yet to be fully ignited.

CHAPTER 5

The Concept of Inclusive Tolerance

The inclusion of immigrants in general and Muslim immigrants in particular is straining liberal democracies in western Europe. From year to year, other issues push themselves to the forefront. As we write, the economic crisis of the Euro zone threatens to undermine the financial foundations of the European Union. Yet even if the crisis is overcome, the inclusion of Muslim immigrants in their new countries will challenge western Europe over the next half century, and if the crisis is not overcome, the challenge of inclusion will be even more daunting. Accordingly, the aim of this chapter is to reexamine—or ironically as it turns out, recover—an earlier and more expansive understanding of tolerance.

To be tolerant, it is now agreed, means to be willing to put up with others that one dislikes or ideas that one disagrees with.[1] And there is good reason to think of tolerance as requiring an effort. What does it take, after all, for a member of a political party to support their own party's right to express its ideas? But for that member to support the right of a party whose ideas they reject and whose success they fear is proof of tolerance. So understood, tolerance is a synonym for toleration.

Toleration has become not merely the primary but also the sole meaning of tolerance as a value in democratic politics. The consequence has been to bury an older understanding of tolerance. The Latin

---

[1] A philosophical tradition stands behind the conception of tolerance. See, for example, Williams 2005. And a body of research—most notably, Sullivan, Piereson, and Marcus 1982—made it the pivotal premise in the measurement of citizens' support for civil liberties and civil rights

root *tolero/are* points the way to a recovery of this older understanding. The first definition strikes the familiar note: "to bear, to endure." But the verb *tolero* encompasses a positive, affirmative, and nurturant disposition, too: "to support, to sustain." This second meaning, though buried over time, has as distinguished a pedigree as the conception of tolerance championed by John Locke and his successors. Thus, in his commentary on the Gallic wars, Caesar expressly uses *tolero* in its positive form: to "support, nourish, maintain, sustain, preserve."[2] Our interest is not in provoking a squabble about definitions. We call attention to this older understanding of tolerance because it points the way to recognizing what contemporary measures of tolerance actually are capturing. It is our claim that in addition to identifying those with ill will toward immigrants, standard measures of anti-immigrant attitudes also identify those whose stance toward immigrants is supportive, affirmative, and inclusive—so much so that they treat immigrants as full members of a common community, and hence our introduction of the concept of inclusive tolerance.

THE CONCEPT OF INCLUSIVE TOLERANCE

Immigrant minorities must overcome many obstacles in making a life for themselves in their new country. It nonetheless is consensually agreed that a major force working against them is the persisting power of prejudice. It is therefore worth being as clear as possible about what constitutes prejudice.

The box "Definitions of Prejudice" presents a number of classic definitions. On a first reading, it is the dissimilarities that stand out. Prejudice is sometimes equated with irrationality (e.g., definitions 3, 4, and 7), sometimes with injustice (definition 10), and sometimes with both (e.g., definitions 1 and 2). Intolerance is sometimes conceived of as an attitude (definitions 1 and 11), and sometimes as the conjunction of an attitude (or emotion) and a pattern of behavior (e.g., definitions 2, 3, 9, and 10). And as if we did not have variety enough already, sometimes prejudice is tied to cognitive simplism in a string of guises, among

---

[2] Lewis 1890. For this display of erudition, we are delighted to acknowledge that we are wholly in debt to our colleague Joshiah Ober.

DEFINITIONS OF PREJUDICE

Definition 1: "Prejudiced attitudes . . . are irrational, unjust, or intolerant dispositions towards others. They are often accompanied by stereotyping. This is the attribution of supposed characteristics of the whole group to all its individual members" (Milner 1975, 9).

Definition 2: "It seems most useful to us to define prejudice as a failure of rationality or a failure of justice or a failure of human-heartedness in an individual's attitude toward members of another ethnic group" (Harding et al. 1969, 6).

Definition 3: "An emotional, rigid attitude, a predisposition to respond to a certain stimulus in a certain way toward a group of people" (Simpson and Yinger 1985, 21).

Definition 4: "Thinking ill of others without sufficient warrant" (Allport 1954, 7).

Definition 5: "Ethnic prejudice is an antipathy based upon a faulty and inflexible generalization. It may be felt or expressed. It may be directed toward a group as a whole or toward an individual because he is a member of that group" (Allport 1954, 9).

Definition 6: "An unsubstantiated prejudgment of an individual or group, favorable or unfavorable in character, tending to action in a consonant direction" (Klineberg 1968, 439).

Definition 7: "A pattern of hostility in interpersonal relations which is directed against an entire group, or against its individual members; it fulfills a specific irrational function for its bearer" (Ackerman and Jahoda 1950, 2–3).

Definition 8: "Hostility or aggression toward individuals on the basis of their group membership" (Buss 1961, 245).

Definition 9: "Group prejudice is now commonly viewed as having two components: hostility and misinformation" (Kelman and Pettigrew 1959, 436).

Definition 10: "A set of attitudes which causes, supports, or justifies discrimination" (Rose 1951, 5).

Definition 11: "An unfavorable attitude toward an object which tends to be highly stereotyped, emotionally charged, and not easily changed by contrary information" (Krech, Crutchfield, and Ballachey 1962).

Note: Adopted from Sniderman et al. 2000, 17.

them stereotypes, misinformation, prejudgment, misinformation, and rigidity (e.g., definitions 3, 4, 6, and 9).

Notwithstanding this conceptual diversity, readers will see a point of commonality in all the definitions of prejudice. People are prejudiced toward members of other groups insofar as they dislike or disdain them by virtue of this fact. And the stronger their hostility toward other groups, the more prejudiced they are. Thus the common strand running through these definitions: "thinking ill of others," "antipathy," "hostility," a "highly charged . . . unfavorable attitude," "a failure of human-heartedness," and "aggression."

Why pick hostility as the attribute to focus on? Why not rigidity, irrationality, or stereotyping, which also appear in a number of definitions? Because cognitive rigidity, irrationality, stereotyping, and other members of this conceptual family spotlight what is going on inside people's heads—in particular, how they process information. But in the study of prejudice and politics, what matters more is how members of a majority group respond to members of a minority group. And hostility picks out a—or as we are willing to argue, *the*—key characteristic of their reactions to minorities: a readiness to injure, push away, deprive, discriminate. In short, prejudice against minorities matters as much as it does because it drives aggression against them.

The all-important questions that previous research on Muslim immigrants in western Europe have addressed are, How much ill will is there toward them, and what can be done to reduce it?

Both remain pressing concerns. The question that we want to ask, though, is whether this is all there is. Is decreasing the level of ill will against minorities and reducing the injuries wrought by it the best that can be hoped for? One of the marks of contemporary liberal democracy is the goodwill many feel toward minorities. Nor is it a matter merely of thinking well of them, or even also wishing them well; it is, crucially, a matter of treating them well. At any rate, that is the hypothesis we propose to test.

What must be true if our hypothesis of goodwill is true? Measures of prejudice are typically conceived of as ordering people in terms of the degree, frequency, or intensity of their negative feelings toward a minority. At one pole are the most negative people, and a continuum stretches out from there, ranging from those who are less negative to those who are still less negative. Though the point is not made explicitly, the people who score the lowest on measures of prejudice are the least negative.

Ordering people from the most to least negative is the task of virtually all measures of prejudice.[3] Thus, measures of anti-Semitism are designed to rank order people from those who most dislike and disdain Jews to those who least dislike and disdain them.[4] Measures of racial prejudice are similarly designed to rank order people from those who most dislike and disdain blacks to those who least do so. And to cite yet one more example, measures of attitudes toward immigrants, including ours, are designed to rank order people from those who most dislike and disdain immigrants to those who least do so. This can be called the unipolar conception of attitudes toward minorities.

But is this the only or indeed right way to think of a continuum of feelings toward minorities? As a thought experiment, consider racial prejudice. The higher a person's score on a measure of racial prejudice, the more negative their feelings toward blacks. Yet what is the meaning of a low score? Surely there are some white Americans with positive attitudes toward black Americans. Insofar as this is so, measures of prejudice order people from those with the most negative attitudes toward blacks to those with the most positive attitudes toward them. We will call this claim that evaluative attitudes toward minorities have a positive as well as negative pole the bipolarity hypothesis.[5]

The bipolarity hypothesis neither requires nor implies symmetry. Likely, fewer members of a majority have positive attitudes toward minorities than hold negative ones. Those who disdain minorities are

---

[3] Research on prejudice as two-dimensional—negative and positive, thereby opening up the possibility of assessing ambivalence—is the noteworthy exception. For a classic work, see Katz, Wackenhut, and Haas 1986. For more recent work, see, for example, Son Hing et al. 2008.

[4] For a classic study of anti-Semitism in the United States, see Selznick and Steinberg 1969.

[5] For empirical evidence, see Sniderman and Stiglitz 2008. Michael Tesler and David O. Sears (2010) expressly make this claim for their measure of racism in their study of the 2008 election. Elisabeth Iversflaten, Scott Blinder, and Robert Ford (2010) provide a complimentary but quite distinct argument. Their studies focus on the internalization of an antiracism norm, and offer an original as well as promising line of reasoning (see also Blinder 2007; Blinder, Ford, and Ivarsflaten 2010). Neither our argument nor our findings are at cross-purposes with theirs. The pivotal distinction is our assertion that there is a positive force, not just a restraint, at work.

quite possibly more inclined to act on their feelings than those who think well of them. Still, it is our claim that a sizable portion of the majority not merely lacks ill will toward minorities but also exhibits goodwill toward them. Thinking well of a minority and even wishing it well are necessary conditions of the older understanding of tolerance that we wish to recover. But they are not sufficient. It is necessary to treat minorities well, too. But what counts as treating them well?

This manifestly is a vexing question in the context of US politics. It has repeatedly been observed that there is consensual support for the principle of equal opportunity, but substantial and sometimes overwhelming opposition to policies to achieve it.[6] This has been dubbed the "principle-policy puzzle," and usually is taken as a sign of either insincerity or hypocrisy. A sober second thought should make it plain that it is anything but a puzzle. The policies to achieve racial equality are liberal ones. Increased funding for government programs to train minorities to be able to compete for jobs is a good example. This aid surely is intended to promote racial equality, and from the perspective of a person on the political left, more government spending and bigger government programs are major tools—not the only ones, but invaluable all the same—to achieve racial equality. But more government spending and bigger government programs are liberal programs. From the perspective of someone on the right, more government spending and bigger government programs are policies that benefit government bureaucrats rather than the people they are meant to help. A different approach is necessary, conservatives believe, one that promotes individual initiative and a willingness to take responsibility for solving one's problems. In short, in a liberal democracy like the United States, what counts as treating minorities well is inherently contestable, because it is inextricably tied to the ongoing competition between liberalism and conservatism as theories of government and citizenship.

At just this point, an advantage of studying the treatment of minorities in a welfare state becomes apparent, given that there is consensus on the assistance that the state should afford members of the national community. Hence, a clear and definite meaning can be given to the question, What counts as treating minorities well? Including them as

---

[6] We rely here on the classic work Schuman et al. 1997.

full members in good standing of the common community. Since inclusion in the community is the criterion, we call a readiness to do so inclusive tolerance.

How people act is a necessary condition of inclusive tolerance. But it is not a sufficient one. Why people do what they do matters, too.[7] Imagine an individual; let's name her A. She is deeply convinced of advanced countries' responsibility for the immiseration of less advanced countries, and views the world as characterized by exploiter and exploited. Does she support benefits being awarded to immigrant minorities? Yes. Is this tolerance, though? No, because she does so to expiate her feelings of guilt. Imagine then another individual, dubbed B. He also supports benefits and rights for immigrants across the board. Yet he does so because of a conviction that they are unequipped to compete in a country whose language and culture is radically different than the country that they came from. It may be proper to describe B as compassionate, empathetic, or patronizing; it would not be proper to portray him as tolerant.

Tolerance is not the same as guilt, compassion, generosity, or noblesse oblige. And although it may suffice in politics to tolerate controversial groups, to be truly tolerant requires more. We surely would not praise a person as racially tolerant merely because they are willing to put up with blacks, despite the fact that they disdain them. The absence of ill will or mere indifference toward Muslim immigrants is not enough; it is necessary to both think well of them and treat them well, too.

Inclusive tolerance thus has two parts: tolerance as an attitude and tolerance as an action. We begin with tolerance as an attitude.

TESTS OF INCLUSIVE TOLERANCE

Positive Affect

A necessary condition of being inclusively tolerant is thinking well of minorities. Our measure of attitudes toward immigrants was not designed to assess a positive affect toward immigrants. It is standard

---

[7] Hibbing and Alford 2004; Zak 2007; Petersen 2012.

issue.[8] All its component items have been used in previous studies—such as beliefs that "foreigners should only be able to receive Danish citizenship after they have learned to act like a Dane" and "if there are not enough jobs, employers should employ Danes ahead of immigrants."[9] It is our claim, however, that this measure orders respondents from those with most negative attitudes toward immigrants to those with the most positive. What therefore must be true if our claim is correct? Those who score low on our attitudes toward immigrants scale must have positive—and *not merely not negative*—attitudes toward Muslims.

To test this assertion, we divided the distribution on the attitudes toward immigrants into (as nearly equal as possible) fifths. The index is constructed so that the higher the score, the more negative the attitude toward immigrants. Table 5.1 therefore shows five columns, with those with the lowest scores on the far left and those with the highest on the far right, followed by a sixth column indicating the scores for all respondents. Our measure of how respondents feel about Muslims could not be more direct. They were presented with a scale running from 0, "Do not like the group at all," to 10, "Like the group very much." The attitudes toward immigrants scale also runs from 0 to 10. For the purposes of comparison, in addition to feelings about Muslims, table 5.1 presents feelings about an array of other groups.

The first row shows the degree to which respondents who differ in their scores on the attitudes toward immigrants scale like Muslims. The columns on the left are labeled "Most positive fifth" and "Second most positive fifth." It is, however, the appropriateness of these labels that is the hypothesis being tested. Are the lowest scorers on the attitudes toward immigrants scale merely the least negative in their feelings about Muslims or are their feelings actually positive? The higher the score, the more positive are the feelings toward Muslims.

The mean score of those who score in the lowest quintile on the attitudes toward immigrants scale, who we have provisionally labeled

---

[8] We introduced this scale in chapter 4; also see appendix D.

[9] It happens that three of the four items are negatively worded, but the direction of the wording is merely a contingent fact: the rejection of an aversive response to a minority is an expression of a positive disposition to them. The construction algorithm is standard issue, too. Just as in previous studies, each item is equally weighted and negative responses are summed.

TABLE 5.1 Group Sympathy by Attitudes toward Immigrants (Scale Scores)

	Attitudes toward immigrants					
	Most positive fifth	Second most positive fifth	Middle fifth	Second most negative fifth	Most negative fifth	All
Muslims	6.89	6.08	5.19	4.03	2.45	5.10
(N = 1,872)	(0.09)	(0.12)	(0.10)	(0.11)	(0.15)	(0.06)
Born-again	3.87	3.97	4.52	4.76	4.74	4.35
Christians	(0.14)	(0.17)	(0.15)	(0.15)	(0.20)	(0.07)
(N = 1,888)						
Far Right	2.03	2.72	3.09	3.65	3.70	2.97
(N = 1,824)	(0.11)	(0.14)	(0.12)	(0.12)	(0.17)	(0.06)
Far Left	4.68	4.17	3.81	3.85	3.65	4.07
(N = 1,833)	(0.13)	(0.14)	(0.12)	(0.12)	(0.16)	(0.06)

Note: Entries are mean scores on a 0–10 scale, with standard errors in parentheses. The question wording is: "I will now mention some of the different groups in Denmark and ask what you think about them. Please respond on a scale from 0 to 10, where 0 indicates that you do not like the group at all, and 10 indicates that you like the group very much." For question wording and scaling of the attitudes toward immigrants scale, see chapter 4 and appendix D. In the table, the scale has been divided into five roughly equal-size categories.

"most positive about Muslims," is 6.89. Moving from the leftmost column to the rightmost one, scores on the like Muslim scale progressively drop. The middle fifth are neutral (5.19), the second most negative fall on the dislike side of the like Muslim scale (4.03), while the most negative fifth in attitudes toward immigrants definitely dislike Muslims (2.45). In short, it is not merely that the feelings about immigrants of those respondents who score low on the attitudes toward immigrants scale are not negative. They are positive.

This result may seem to close the question—low scorers on the attitudes toward immigrants scale do not merely dislike immigrants; they like them. But the feelings of like or dislike that respondents express about immigrants, in isolation, are systematically ambiguous. Low scores on the attitudes toward immigrants scale may pick out people who have positive feelings about Muslims specifically. Alternatively, low scores may select the type of person who tends to have positive feelings toward others in general. Consider the second row in table 5.1, which shows respondents' feelings about born-again Christians. All in all, they are liked less than Muslims. The crucial point, though, is this: those who score low on the attitudes toward immigrants scale like Muslims strikingly more than they like born-again Christians (the mean scores are 6.89 compared to 3.87).[10]

Why is this point critical? Because it reveals that when low scorers on the attitudes toward immigrants scale report that they like Muslims, it is not because they are prone to saying that they like everyone. The last two rows on the spectrum of scores in table 5.1 complete this more differentiated portrait of those who are tolerant of immigrants. On the one hand, they are more likely than high scorers to dislike the far Right. On the other hand, they are more likely than high scorers to like the far Left. Indeed, the striking feature of table 5.1 is that those we classify as tolerant like Muslims far more than they like born-again Christians, the far Left, or the far Right. Even putting it this way understates the point. They feel perfectly free to express their dislike of some other groups. It is Muslims, and Muslims alone, that they express a clear feeling of liking. We therefore will treat those scoring low on the attitudes toward immigrants scale as not merely lacking in negative attitudes toward immigrants but instead having positive ones. They qualify as tolerant rather than simply as not intolerant—as having goodwill toward immigrants and not merely as lacking ill will.

But there is all the difference between thinking well of immigrants and treating them well. Evidence of what people do, not just how they feel, is required, or still more specifically, proof not just of a desire to be inclusive of immigrants but in fact acting to include them. That is the task we turn to now.

Civil Rights

All who legally reside in Denmark, by virtue of residence alone, are entitled to fundamental civil rights. Freedom of expression is one; freedom of assembly another. It is one thing, though, for members of a minority to be entitled to rights. It is another for citizens to line up on their side in

[10] It is, of course, just the other way around for those who score high on the attitudes toward immigrants scale. They dislike Muslims markedly more they than they dislike born-again Christians (2.45 compared to 4.74).

support of their rights A basic test of inclusive tolerance, then, is inclusion of immigrants in the community of citizens entitled to civil rights.

How can we determine whether those we have classified as tolerant not merely wish immigrants to be treated well but actually treat them well, too—are protective, supportive, and inclusive? Earlier, we introduced a measure of commitment to civil rights. This measure summarizes decisions made about entitlement to rights. People are asked, for example, whether Muslims have a right to make presentations to high school students and take part in public debates and to (not) have their phones tapped by police. For convenience, we split the distribution on our scale of commitment to civil rights into arithmetic thirds. Table 5.2 shows the percentage scoring in the highest third of the commitment to civil rights scale as a function of how positive or negative their attitudes are concerning immigrants.

Consider how the most positive fifth deals with Muslims: 93 percent score high on our scale of commitment to civil rights. The level of support among the second most positive fifth, though lower, is still high in absolute terms: 77 percent score high on the scale of commitment to civil rights. Then, the pattern we saw in table 5.1 further repeats itself: there is less than majority support among the second most negative fifth, and far less than majority support among the most negative fifth.

It is only to be expected that levels of support for civil rights for a controversial group—whether Muslim or any other group—will be higher for those who like the group and lower for those who dislike it. Our interest lies with two other questions. The first is whether our measure of attitudes toward immigrants is merely a measure of how much people like or dislike immigrants. It clearly is at least this, as the results in table 5.1 depicted. But we believe it is not merely this. It also is a measure of tolerance—a willingness to consider members of another ethnic, political, or social group to be members in good standing of the national community as well. Presuming that the answer to the first question is yes, then a second question presents itself. The more socially tolerant are naturally more likely than the socially intolerant to support the civil rights of Muslims. Yet are the more socially tolerant as likely to support the rights of Muslims as they are to support the civil rights of fellow Danes?

TABLE 5.2 Inclusive Tolerance and Civil Rights (Percent in Highest Third of Supporters of Civil Rights)

	Attitudes toward immigrants					
	Most positive fifth	Second most positive fifth	Middle fifth	Second most negative fifth	Most negative fifth	All
Muslims (N = 456)	93%	77%	62%	48%	29%	66%
Born-again Christians (N = 462)	84%	73%	55%	52%	36%	62%
Far Right (N = 506)	80%	60%	55%	41%	40%	57%
Far Left (N = 427)	91%	80%	62%	43%	24%	65%

Note: Entries are the percentage in each category of attitudes toward immigrants who fall in the most supportive third on the scale of support for the groups' civil rights. For question wordings for civil rights, see table 2.2. For question wording and scaling of the attitudes toward immigrants scale, see chapter 4 and appendix D. In the table, the scale has been divided into five roughly equal-size categories.

Again the answer is yes. Virtually all the most positive fifth of the socially tolerant score in the top tier of supporters of civil liberties, or more precisely, 93 percent do. Looking at the details in table 5.2, that number is higher than the numbers scoring in the top tier of supporters of civil liberties for born-again Christians and the far Right. But to point to these differences is to pick at details. The most positive fifth and even the second most positive fifth give overwhelming support to the civil rights of all out-of-the-mainstream groups, with the arguable exception of the far Right. In terms of civil rights, the inclusively tolerant indeed include out-of-the-mainstream groups, encompassing Muslims just as much as Danes, as members of a common community, treating them just as they would treat a fellow Dane.

Focusing now on the negative pole of the attitudes toward immigrants scale, again picking at details, one could attempt an argument that Muslims received less support for their rights than, say, born-again Christians and the far Right. But the differences are small, and the big point is that the level of support for civil rights and liberties systematically falls, for all groups, from a high level at the positive pole of tolerance to a low level, again for all groups, at the negative pole of tolerance. Second, low scorers on the attitudes toward immigrants scale are inclusively tolerant in the most straightforward sense: they give overwhelming support to the civil rights and civil liberties of Muslims. Indeed, they offer so much support that they treat Muslims as members of a common community, supporting their rights as fully as they support those of fellow Danes.

Now we turn to a final criterion: the full inclusion of Muslims as members of the welfare state.

Inclusive Tolerance and Welfare Benefits

The premise of Danes' understanding of the welfare state is that they are partners in a moral covenant. It is as partners that they form a common community, not merely a nationl state. Accordingly, inclusive tolerance in its broadest terms turns on the degree to which *immigrant minorities are treated as fellow members of a community that takes responsibility for the welfare of its members*. But treated as fellow members with respect to what?

In a welfare state, the question of with respect to what has a clear answer. To be treated as a full member of a common community is to be awarded all the benefits of the welfare state awarded to members of the larger community by virtue of their being members of a common community. This standard is easily met in a welfare state like Denmark. The right to claim a benefit may be universal, but the right itself is not unconditional. People in need are not entitled to welfare benefits merely by virtue of being in need of them. They must earn the right. As important, there is a shared understanding in Danish society of what people must do to have earned these benefits. They must make a sincere effort to contribute to the welfare of the community before they are entitled to social welfare benefits themselves. In the Danish political idiom, as we have remarked, duties come before rights.

The activation policy is a prize example. The objective of this policy, readers will recall, is to facilitate finding a regular job. People receiving social welfare benefits are required to accept temporary jobs or take part in job training programs.[11] This policy is an instance of government

---

[11] See the discussion of the tougher requirements experiment in chapter 3.

efforts to enforce the social covenant underpinning the welfare state, and—though honored more in the breach than in practice—provide citizens with the skills and support they need to meet their obligations to the welfare state.[12]

The activation policy—happily for investigators of prejudice and discrimination, yet less so for their victims—developed a subtext. At the outset, the argument for the activation policy was a general one: the need to create economic incentives for people on welfare to find a job. But the center-right government, with the assistance of the Danish People's Party, tied the problem of moving people in general off welfare and into work to immigrants in particular. In 2005, the Danish government launched the initiative "A New Chance for Everyone" with the aim of improving the integration of immigrants. A significant part of this initiative was preoccupied with the high unemployment rates among immigrants. The government sought to lower the economic incentives for receiving welfare benefits, and hence, force welfare recipients to make an effort to find a job. Instructively, however, the initiative did not simply lower the rate of social welfare benefits in general. Rather, it specifically lowered the benefits for two narrow groups of recipients: individuals permanently on social welfare and couples on social welfare. The government was quite explicit about the intentions behind this targeting, noting, for example, that "the proposition will especially provide immigrants with improved incentives for taking a job, because they constitute the majority of couples on social welfare."[13] In our experiments, we exploit these background beliefs, using them to provide a credible justification for imposing tougher requirements on immigrants. Our conception of inclusive tolerance in this respect incorporates the spirit of the standard notion of tolerance: members of the majority should have to resist some temptation to treat minorities differently and worse.

The activation policy, by providing a credible justification, imposes more severe requirements on immigrants, thereby opening the door to discrimination. The readiness to walk through this door, we have contended, turns on the difference between the logic of retrospective versus prospective judgments. It is self-contradictory to claim that a young

[12] See Cox 2001; Loftager 2004, 93–95. As we described in chapter 3, job training activities are routinely accused of being both dull and meaningless.

[13] Danish Government 2005, 27 (our translation).

person has not met their duty since, by virtue of being young, it is questionable whether they will do so. As such, everyone supports the same assistance to young immigrants as to fellow Danes, and the same stricter requirements on young Danes as on immigrants. Decisions dealing with older immigrants, in contrast, allow the logic of retrospective judgments to come into play. One may take account of the likelihood that a person wishing to receive a benefit has done their duty to contribute to the larger society, thus opening the door to drawing on perceptions that immigrants have shirked their responsibility to the larger society.

The conditional mood "may" points toward another condition for discriminatory behavior. A common perception of Muslim women is that they choose—or are required—to stay at home rather than go out and participate in the life of the larger society. They therefore wind up enjoying social welfare benefits while conforming to Muslim customs that sequester women from males outside the family. Yet whether members of the majority draw on this perception depends on whether they are disposed to do so; if they dislike immigrants, they will hold to this view of Muslim women. But what should we expect if they do not dislike immigrants, or still better, if they do not merely not dislike them but instead think well of them and wish them well? It is not as though a person who is well disposed toward Muslim immigrants will be ignorant of the perception that a Muslim woman has not worked in the labor force to the same extent as an older Danish woman is likely to have done. The view of Muslim women choosing or being required to stay at home is not an entirely imaginative action—which is, for our purposes, precisely the point. Because this perception of older Muslim women is reality oriented, it is not implausible to suppose that some effort is required to set it aside. Not implausible, we say, because we have no way of providing direct evidence to test this conjecture. Then again, to say not implausible is, for an American at any rate, to put our case too weakly. Jesse Jackson, at the peak of his fame as a leader in the civil rights movement, once famously remarked: "There is nothing more painful to me at this stage in my life than to walk down the street and hear footsteps and start thinking about robbery. Then look around and see somebody White and feel relieved."[14]

[14] Quoted in Arkes and Tetlock 2004, 257.

Then again, this story underestimates the opportunity that our experiments provide to treat immigrants differently or worse. Respondents are asked either about an immigrant or native citizen. They are not put in the position, at one and the same moment, of showing that they treat the one worse than the other. So we will interpret an older immigrant being treated the same as a fellow Dane, in the face of a credible justification for not doing so, as an affirmative act.

Table 5.3 displays support for the imposition of tougher requirements on a woman depending on whether she has an immigrant background or not for each quintile of scorers on the attitudes toward immigrants scale. Consider first the rightmost column, which summarizes the reactions of those with the most negative attitudes toward immigrants. These respondents are about twice as willing to impose stricter activation requirements on the immigrant woman than on the nonimmigrant one (with mean scores of 0.76 compared to 0.41). No less striking is how deep into the general population discriminatory behavior goes. Columns three, four, and five in table 5.3 account for roughly 60 percent of our sample.[15] Each shows a double standard, with immigrants treated differently and worse. This evidence of ill will should be kept clearly in mind as we now turn to the question of goodwill.

Inclusive tolerance goes beyond toleration, we are arguing. It also goes beyond wishing minorities well to actually treating them well. One standard of treating immigrants well—not the only one, to be clear, but the one that we believe bears most directly on immigrants becoming a part of their new communities—is their being treated as members of the community. In this light, consider the first column in table 5.3. The most tolerant are far less willing to line up in support of imposing stricter requirements on the immigrant woman in her fifties than are any of the other groups—indeed, they are only half as likely to do so as the most intolerant (with mean scores of 0.39 compared to 0.76). Still more to the point, the most tolerant are equally reluctant to impose tougher requirements on the nonimmigrant woman, but they are not more so. In fact, they respond to the immigrant woman the same way that they respond to the nonimmigrant woman in the

---

[15] Which is a quite different thing from asserting that 60 percent of our sample, and by inference the general population, discriminates against immigrants.

TABLE 5.3 Tougher Requirements Experiment: Support for Tougher Requirements for Receiving Welfare Payments by Attitudes toward Immigrants

	Attitudes toward immigrants				
	Most positive fifth	Second most positive fifth	Middle fifth	Second most negative fifth	Most negative fifth
Woman in her fifties (N = 340)	0.37 (0.04)	0.49 (0.06)	0.47 (0.05)	0.50 (0.04)	0.41 (0.07)
Immigrant woman in her fifties (N = 331)	0.39 (0.05)	0.52 (0.06)	0.57 (0.05)	0.66 (0.04)	0.76 (0.06)

Note: Entries are mean support for tougher requirements for receiving welfare payments, measured on a 0–1 scale, with standard errors in parentheses. Higher values indicate greater support for tougher requirements. Question wording: "Imagine a woman in her fifties [with an immigrant background] who is currently on welfare. To what extent do you agree or disagree that the activation requirement for her should be made stricter?" One version included the bracketed part, while the other version excluded it. The response categories were: agree completely, agree somewhat, neither agree nor disagree, disagree somewhat, and disagree completely. "Don't know" responses were excluded. For question wording and scaling of the attitudes toward immigrants scale, see chapter 4 and appendix D. In the table, the scale has been divided into five roughly equal-size categories.

same circumstances (0.39 compared to 0.37). And as an inspection of the second column of table 5.3 reveals, the same is true of the scorers in the second most positive quintile: they are as supportive of an immigrant woman in her fifties as of a fellow Dane in her fifties (0.52 compared to 0.49).

Our measures of tolerance are crude, we acknowledge—although, we would add, no more so than those of previous studies. But our results are more reliable than those of previous public opinion surveys, thanks to the power of randomized experiments.[16] We believe that the results of the woman in her fifties version of the tougher requirements experiment suggest two conclusions. First, immigrants are treated as fellow members of a common community by a substantial portion of the public, on the order of four in ten. Second, in the rest of society there is

[16] Which is not to suggest that each particular survey experiment does not suffer the standard limitations of survey research.

compelling evidence of discriminatory behavior toward immigrants.[17] We think it is fair to say that the first conclusion will come as more of a surprise to researchers than the second. Who doubts that prejudice and discrimination are problems? Yet to our knowledge, previous research has not focused on the opposite side of the coin: that substantial numbers treat minorities as members of a common community. So it is our good fortune that the hypothesis of inclusive tolerance can be put to the test in a second and altogether independent experiment.

In the many children experiment, we asked respondents whether the welfare benefits of a family where both parents are on welfare and have children should be reduced in order to press them to find a job. Randomly, the family was described as an "immigrant" family half of the time. The rationale behind the experiment was, obviously enough, to trigger the widely held view that immigrants are disproportionately on welfare and do not practice family planning.

Table 5.4 presents the results of a parallel analysis of the many children experiment. The results buttress both conclusions that we drew from the woman in her fifties experiment. First, even a cursory glance at columns three, four, or five will reveal evidence of discrimination. The odds that an immigrant family where both parents are on welfare and have many children will have their welfare benefits cut are dramatically higher than for a nonimmigrant family in exactly the same circumstances. To look at those in the middle quintile—to point to a striking example—the mean level of support for cutting the welfare benefits of an immigrant family with many children is 0.56; in contrast, the mean level for doing the same to a Danish family with many children is only 0.41.

Again, we urge keeping this finding of discrimination squarely in mind. But without minimizing the importance of this finding, we also contend in our hypothesis that attitudes toward minorities can be positive rather than merely not negative. Hence, we want to underscore the second finding in table 5.4. The lower the score, the less support for cutting welfare benefits. An inspection of columns one and two shows

[17] We cannot determine the proportion of the public that discriminates, partly because of the specific design of our experiments, and partly because it will vary from situation to situation. More specifically, our experiments are between—rather than within—subjects, and our measures are ordinal, not ratio.

TABLE 5.4 Many Children Experiment: Support for Cutting Welfare Benefits
by Attitudes toward Immigrants

	Attitudes toward immigrants				
	Most positive fifth	Second most positive fifth	Middle fifth	Second most negative fifth	Most negative fifth
Family with many children (N = 490)	0.24 (0.03)	0.29 (0.05)	0.41 (0.04)	0.50 (0.04)	0.65 (0.05)
Immigrant family with many children (N = 461)	0.21 (0.03)	0.35 (0.05)	0.56 (0.04)	0.69 (0.03)	0.81 (0.04)

Note: Entries are mean support for cutting welfare payments, measured on a 0–1 scale, with standard errors in parentheses. Higher values indicate cutting welfare payments. Question wording: "Imagine [a family/an immigrant family] with many children, where both the mother and father are on welfare. To what extent do you agree or disagree that their welfare should be reduced in order to push them to find a job?" One version included the "family" and the other included the "immigrant family" part of the bracket. The response categories were: agree completely, agree somewhat, neither agree nor disagree, disagree somewhat, and disagree completely. "Don't know" responses were excluded. For question wording and scaling of the attitudes toward immigrants scale, see chapter 4 and appendix D. In the table, the scale has been divided into five roughly equal-size categories.

that those with positive attitudes treat immigrants and fellow Danes alike. To be sure, visually there are appearances of difference. Those with the most positive attitudes toward immigrants may seem to favor them (0.21 versus 0.24); those with the second most positive attitudes seem to favor fellow Danes (0.35 versus 0.29). But the appearance of differences is visual: statistically, the differences are insignificant. The many children experiment, then, replicates the finding of inclusive tolerance—immigrants being treated as fellow members of the community by a substantial portion of ordinary citizens—in the woman in her fifties experiment.

Demonstrating that results are consistent with one's hypothesis is only half the battle, however. It also is necessary to establish that they are not consistent with alternative (plausible) hypotheses. We therefore turn to testing alternative explanations of our results.

Two Competing Hypotheses

Two alternative explanations stand out. The first is partisan ideology. Parties on the left are programmatically more supportive of immigrants, more sensitive to the hurdles of adjustment in a new country that they must overcome, and in any case more committed to state action to help those who are less well off, which very much includes large numbers of Muslim immigrants in a country like Denmark. In contrast, parties on the right are programmatically committed to making the welfare state more efficient and thus more affordable, more heavily weight the disproportionate demands that immigrants are putting on the welfare state, and are in any case more likely to perceive immigrants as posing a threat to the country's culture and traditions.

Partisan ideology is being invoked in a minor key, we would emphasize. It goes too far to assert that the ordinary citizen is "innocent of ideology, ill prepared, and perhaps even incapable of following (much less actually participating in) discussions about the direction that government take."[18] This is no doubt true, if ideological thinking is pitched at a high enough level of abstraction or sufficiently challenging degree of complexity. But that is not the level at which an ideological dimension like libertarianism-authoritarianism is pitched.[19] It requires no mastery of political concepts to hold to a view that violent crimes should be punished more severely or economic growth should be ensured even at the cost of environmental interests. It surely also cannot be doubted that adherents of parties on the right are markedly less likely to believe that immigrants deserve government aid than adherents of parties on the left. And it cannot be doubted for good reason. As it turns out, our measures of partisan ideology and attitudes toward immigrants are tied together ($r = 0.42$, $p < 0.001$). Yet if the two are so strongly correlated, then it is all the more plausible to suppose that partisan ideology, not tolerance, is carrying the explanatory burden.

A competing account runs along social psychological rather than political lines. A long established line of research has illuminated the

---

[18] Kinder 2003, 13.
[19] For an analysis putting principles and values center stage in citizen political reasoning, see Goren 2013.

far-reaching consequences of interpersonal trust.[20] Trust supplies both the assurance and incentive for social cooperation. From this analytic perspective, a readiness to trust and think well of immigrants is a generalization of a readiness to trust and think well of people in general. Insofar as this is so, positive attitudes toward immigrants will only appear to encourage the evenhanded treatment of immigrants. In reality, the root of evenhandedness is interpersonal trust. This is the generalized trust hypothesis, which has good empirical credentials, too. Our generalized social trust scale correlates highly with our attitudes toward immigrants scale ($r = -0.42$, $p < 0.001$).[21] And to the degree that attitudes toward immigrants are a function of interpersonal trust, the evenhanded treatment of immigrants and native Danes may be grounded not in attitudes toward immigrants specifically but instead in attitudes toward people generally.

The inclusive tolerance hypothesis, as we have seen, provides an account of evenhandedness. Can the two competing hypotheses do so as well? Table 5.5 reports the results of testing the partisan ideology hypothesis, first, in the many children experiment and then in the woman in her fifties version of the tougher requirements experiment.[22]

The upper panel of table 5.5 presents the results of the many children experiment. The difference in reactions to immigrant and Danish families with many children is arithmetically smaller for the Left and nonexistent for the Social Liberal Party. Strictly, however, to obtain a statistically significant difference between the ideological Left and Right requires combining the Social Liberal Party with the avowedly Left parties, which seems a tad arbitrary, and in any case provides not nearly as satisfactory an account of evenhandedness as the inclusive tolerance hypothesis.[23]

---

[20] Kumlin and Rothstein 2005; Putnam 2000; Sønderskov 2011; Uslaner 2002.

[21] The generalized social trust scale consists of three items: "There are not that many people you can trust completely," "Other people will exploit you if you are not careful," and "Now I would like to hear whether you think you can trust most people or if you think that you can't be too careful when dealing with other people (you can trust most people/it depends . . . / you can't be too careful when dealing with other people)." The scale was constructed such that higher values indicate higher interpersonal trust; see appendix D.

[22] Note that this table is a replication of the results from tables 3.5 and 3.6 in chapter 3.

[23] The results are available on request.

TABLE 5.5 A Test of the Partisan Ideology Hypothesis

	Left wing	Social Liberals	Social Democrats	Center-Right	Danish People's Party
Many children experiment					
Family with	0.19	0.30	0.33	0.52	0.53
many children	(0.04)	(0.05)	(0.04)	(0.03)	(0.06)
(N = 431)					
Immigrant	0.25	0.27	0.46	0.67	0.72
family with	(0.05)	(0.05)	(0.04)	(0.03)	(0.06)
many children					
(N = 399)					
Tougher requirements experiment					
Woman in	0.37	0.46	0.35	0.51	0.38
her fifties	(0.07)	(0.07)	(0.04)	(0.04)	(0.07)
(N = 293)					
Immigrant	0.56	0.54	0.56	0.61	0.67
woman in	(0.06)	(0.07)	(0.05)	(0.04)	(0.07)
her fifties					
(N = 293)					

Note: Entries are mean support for cutting welfare payments or mean support for tougher requirements for receiving welfare payments, respectively, measured on a 0–1 scale, with standard errors in parentheses. Higher values indicate greater support. For question wordings, see tables 5.3 and 5.4.

Perhaps the partisan ideology fares better in the woman in her fifties experiment. The results in the lower panel of table 5.5 make plain the answer: no. Across the ideological spectrum, there is clear and distinct evidence of a double standard. For parties on the left, the readiness to impose tougher requirements on an immigrant woman in her fifties is 0.56, compared to 0.37 if she is nonimmigrant. For Social Democrats, the comparable figures are 0.56 compared to 0.35, and for the Center-Right, 0.51 and 0.61.

The upper panel of table 5.6 presents the test results of the generalized trust hypothesis in the two experiments. Again we begin with the many children experiment. At each level of trust, there is more support for requiring immigrant families with many children to be cut off welfare than their Danish counterparts. What is more, the level of discrimination is essentially the same at all levels of trust (low trust is 0.56 and 0.69, respectively; high trust is 0.27 and 0.35, respectively). And as the

TABLE 5.6 A Test of the Generalized Trust Hypothesis

	Low trust	Middle trust	High trust
Many children experiment			
Family with many children	0.55	0.41	0.27
(N = 490)	(0.03)	(0.03)	(0.03)
Immigrant family with many	0.69	0.53	0.35
children (N = 461)	(0.03)	(0.03)	(0.03)
Tougher requirements experiment			
Woman in her fifties	0.49	0.39	0.46
(N = 293)	(0.04)	(0.04)	(0.04)
Immigrant woman in her	0.62	0.60	0.51
fifties (N = 293)	(0.04)	(0.04)	(0.04)

Note: Entries are mean support for cutting welfare payments or mean support for tougher requirements for receiving welfare payments, respectively, measured on a 0–1 scale, with standard errors in parentheses. Higher values indicate greater support. For question wording, see tables 5.3 and 5.4. For question wording and scaling of the generalized social trust scale, see text and appendix D. In the table, the scale has been divided into three roughly equal-size categories.

lower panel of table 5.6 shows, the generalized trust hypothesis fails to clear the fence in the woman in her fifties version of the tougher requirements experiment. Again, there is more support for imposing tougher requirements to receive social benefits on an immigrant than on a Danish woman at all levels of generalized trust, and again, too, the degree of discrimination is indistinguishable at all levels of generalized trust (low trust is 0.49 and 0.62, respectively; high trust is 0.46 and 0.51, respectively).

In short, as the results of both the many children and woman in her fifties experiments show, neither the partisan ideology or generalized trust hypotheses provide as satisfactory an account of evenhandedness, let alone a superior one, as the hypothesis of inclusive tolerance.

CODA

Tolerance once was regarded as the sine qua non of democratic politics. No longer. It has been demoted from the first rank of democratic values by many theorists of democracy. It is no better than a second-rank value—or "mere" tolerance, as they often refer to it. Why mere tolerance? Because it sets the bar too low, theorists argue. In an age of diversity and multiculturalism, the argument now runs, every group has a duty not merely to accept but also to respect and indeed esteem the lifeways of other groups.

For our part, we have become persuaded that tolerance is an underrated value—underrated because what it is taken to mean is constricted. Tolerance is not a synonym for toleration. It goes beyond a willingness to put up with others whose beliefs, appearance, or origins differ. It involves not merely the absence of ill will but also the presence of goodwill. We are far from supposing that this disposition to think of and treat minorities well is equal in strength to the array of opposing forces. But the results we have reported give credibility to a claim that substantial numbers think well of minorities, wish them well, and treat them well, too. This is a form of tolerance that is, above all else, inclusive, embracing immigrants and treating them as fellow members of a common community.

CHAPTER 6

The Democratic Impulse

Ours is a study of one country, over a fairly brief period of time—on the order of four months—during a political crisis. Still, at every point where direct comparison is possible, the results of our research have agreed with the findings of previous research.[1] And on key points where our procedures are new, the results of a follow-up experiment replicate those of the initial experiment. So with the appropriate qualifications and caveats, we want to put down the broader lessons we ourselves have drawn from our specific results.

A DEFENSE OF MUSLIM RIGHTS

There is a large literature on democratic lamentation. Two of the keenest laments are intertwined: intolerance is an irrepressible force in the popular culture and the commitment of citizens to the core values of a democratic politics is superficial. There is a superfluity of evidence of how readily citizens deny fundamental political rights to groups they perceive to be threatening, and how readily they perceive controversial

---

[1] For example, consistent with previous research, the analysis over time of the three surveys we conducted documented the restraining influence of elites, both political and social. Also, consistent with previous research, the level of support for the civil liberties of Muslims and Islamic fundamentalists is correlated with the degree to which each is perceived to be a threat. Finally, and again consistent with previous research, when we repeated previous analyses of the ideological sources of hostility to immigration, our results duplicated the findings of previous studies.

groups to be threatening.[2] It is against this background that the most striking finding of this study should be set.

The Cartoon Crisis, notwithstanding its self-deprecating appellation, was the fiercest political storm to strike Denmark since the Second World War. It hit against a background in which voters' anger and resentment toward immigrants had become a major force in Danish politics. Inside Denmark, publicly prominent imams like Sheikh Hlayhel declared that "democracy as practiced in Denmark is worth nothing to Muslims."[3] Outside Denmark, Muslim leaders posted bounties for assassinations, organized protest demonstrations of hundreds of thousands of people, initiated boycotts against Danish goods, and stood aside or applauded while mobs attacked Danish embassies. On the other side of the divide, some Danish politicians did not hold back either. Pia Kjærsgaard, leader of the Danish People's Party, declared—in a written essay for a newsletter, mind you, not an impromptu speech—that

> the harmful effects of immigration have reached a level that would have shocked a Dane a hundred years ago to see the Middle Ages return. Not in their wildest dreams would they have imagined (in 1900) that large neighborhoods in Copenhagen and other Danish cities in 2005 would be populated by people at a lower step of civilization, with imported primitive and cruel customs like honor killings, forced marriage, Halal slaughter, and blood feud. Because this is exactly what has happened: that thousands and thousands of people who seem to be stuck in 1005, not 2005—in terms of civilization, culturally and spiritually—have come to a country that left the Middle Ages behind hundreds of years ago.[4]

For that matter, the government stage-managed its political response, striking self-serving postures ostensibly—and ostentatiously—in defense of Danish values, while refusing to do what it easily could have done, such as agreeing to courtesy meetings with Muslim leaders, which it could easily have carried off without compromising the principle of freedom of thought and expression. Instead, its dominant response

---

[2] For exceptions, see Davis 2007; Nunn, Crockett, and William 1978. But see also Brooks and Manza 2013; Marcus et al. 1995; Sullivan, Piereson, and Marcus 1982.

[3] Quoted in Klausen 2009, 87.

[4] June 13, 2005, quoted in Seidenfaden and Larsen 2006, 224–25.

was to ratchet up the tension of the crisis. Meet with Muslims who were concerned about the cartoons? Absolutely not, the prime minister declared. "You cannot apologize for something you have not done," he said.[5] And the public mood toward Islamic fundamentalists was almost universal fear and anger.

There was a superabundance of tinder and no shortage of matches. Yet what was the most significant finding of our study? Ordinary citizens maintained a solid wall of support for the civil rights and civil liberties of Muslims. And we mean both solid and wall. Just as decisive a majority supported the civil liberties of Muslims as supported those of born-again Christians. This finding, if valid, is important. It should encourage moderate political leaders. It should give assurance to Muslim immigrants that they have a greater measure of protection than they might reasonably suppose. It should challenge students of politics to have more faith in the capacity of citizens to meet the responsibilities of democratic citizenship.

A wall of support for the civil liberties and civil rights of Muslims, even in the face of a rage of demands by Muslims that Muslim values take precedence over Danish values—that is the most important finding of our study. We have confidence in this finding because of our measurement procedures. Those who were asked about Muslims were not asked about Islamic fundamentalists or born-again Christians, and vice versa. Those who were asked about one of the groups could not possibly know that others were asked about the other group, so no one had any reason to skew their answers to ensure that how they responded to one group would be consistent with how they responded to the other. There were multiple measures of support for civil rights and civil liberties. And most crucial by the length of many football fields, the evidence of popular defense of Muslims is the product of not mere observation but rather genuine experiments. The group that people were asked about was decided on a purely random basis. Those who were asked about the rights of Muslims and those asked about the rights of born-again Christians were therefore the same in all respects, unobservable as well as observable, chance differences aside. This finding of a defense of Muslim rights thus gives some reason for a measure of faith in the democratic experiment.

[5] Quoted in Klausen 2009, 32.

Why, then, the divergence—or is it too much to call it a contradiction?—between the (relatively) optimistic picture of democratic citizenship that our results suggest and the decidedly pessimistic conclusion that the findings of previous studies have supported?

It is not because the attitudes of Danes toward Muslims are unique. Muslims and immigrants are for all practical purposes synonyms, and we have seen that the attitudes of Danes toward immigrants are not in any appreciable degree more positive, or negative, than those of the Dutch, English, French, and Germans.[6] Nor is it because Danes have an unconditional commitment to the political rights of controversial groups. On the contrary, we have seen that Danes are perfectly capable of opposing the political rights of a number of groups—Islamic fundamentalists among them.[7] Is it, perhaps, the unusual circumstances of our study? Possibly, but crises over the rights of minorities tend to undercut, not reinforce, support for the rights of minorities. Are our results, then, evidence not of citizens' commitments but rather of the influence of political elites? Yes, political elites ran a top-down campaign in support of freedom of expression, and support for free speech was highest when elite influence was strongest. But we saw that regardless of whether political elites mobilized in support of free speech or not, Danes gave as solid support to the rights of Muslims as to those of born-again Christians—a group whose legitimacy in Danish society cannot be disputed—regardless of elite influence.

Why then, to ask again, the divergence between our (relatively) optimistic picture of democratic citizenship and the decidedly pessimistic one of previous research? It is partly a matter of perspective, as we mean now to make plain, but in addition, it is partly because the impression of optimism can be misleading: the strengths are genuine, yet they entail equally genuine weaknesses.

THE CATEGORIZATION PARADOX

Most studies of political tolerance start with what goes on in people's heads—for example, identifying groups that people perceive to be threatening and then demonstrating that support for civil liberties is

---

[6] See table 2.1.

[7] See table 2.3.

lower for those groups. This internal investigation is an integral part of understanding the bases and dynamics of political tolerance. It is nonetheless our claim that the most useful starting point is what goes on outside their heads: What are the groups whose civil liberties citizens are being asked to support like?

All groups that potentially face a challenge to their civil liberties are controversial. The groups that we studied differ in many ways. Some are expressly political, and others not. Some are religious, and others not. Some are Danish, and some not. Some have shown themselves to pose a clear and distinct threat to public safety and order, and most not. All these differences are potential bases for categorization, and the last, whether there is good reason to associate a group with violence or the threat of violence, may seem the prime candidate in deciding whether a group is entitled to civil liberties or not.

In fact, our results indicate that the key to categorization is whether the actions of a group show that it accepts the rules of the larger society. The group may be critical of the practices of the larger society—even intensely critical. But provided they are critics, not adversaries, there is a general readiness to support their rights. As noted earlier, we characterized this category of groups as out of the mainstream. In contrast, other groups are not merely critical of the practices of the larger society but also have pitted themselves against it, and if the group—not all its members to be sure, yet a significant number and typically the most publicly visible—has violated the rules of the larger society, there will be a reluctance to support its rights. We called this category of groups, as discussed before, transgressive.

The largest number of citizens make use of these categories—out of the mainstream and transgressive—more than other ones, and we know this not because they say so but instead because they sort groups into categories that mirror the distinction between the two. Born-again Christians, the far Left, and the far Right are categorized as out-of-the-mainstream groups, and we know this because they are treated alike. Similarly, the Autonome, bikers, and neo-Nazis are categorized as transgressive groups, and we know this because they, too, are treated alike.[8]

---

[8] The categorization of neo-Nazis is especially instructive, since it allows us to distinguish between categorization on the basis of a group being transgressive and categorization on the basis of a group being threatening. Most Danes view neo-Nazis as anathema, but neo-Nazis do not remotely match the Autonome's and bikers' records of rioting and

This classification scheme does not require an out-of-the-ordinary level of interest in politics to grasp, still less a sophisticated understanding of democratic values. It is simple; it is grounded in the publicly visible acts of groups—or rather, their most prominent leaders—and hence, widely agreed on and easy to follow. To be sure, not all citizens follow this classification scheme, but the majority of them do so—with counterintuitive consequences.

There was a witches' brew of suspicion, anger, resentment, and contempt for Muslim immigrants *before* the crisis. Toss in the attacks on Danish embassies, foreign imams issuing death fatwas, and Middle Eastern governments demanding that respect for the prophet Mohammed take precedence over the values of liberal democracy, and the outcome appeared foreordained—a backlash against Muslims. But there was no backlash. And there was no backlash because Muslims in Denmark are not transgressive. They do not act as adversaries; they do not pit themselves against the larger society. That was true before the crisis. It was true, strikingly, throughout the crisis. Muslims did not hold mass marches and demonstrations during the crisis denouncing Denmark and its values. They respect the same boundaries as most Danes, and Danes recognize this. So Danes put them in the same category as other groups whose beliefs are out of the mainstream, and notwithstanding the feelings of many of them, stood as solidly behind their rights as they did behind those of born-again Christians—by any criterion, a manifestly legitimate group in Danish society.

The defense of the core democratic rights of Muslims is evidence of an unexpected degree of strength within liberal democracies.[9] But

---

violence, and are in no serious sense a threat to safety or order. Still, neo-Nazis are manifestly transgressive, and so they are grouped with other transgressive groups—most obviously, the Autonome and Hell's Angels.

[9] It is this support for core democratic rights—freedom of speech most notably—that we have investigated. The War on Terror has rightly raised concerns about the public's reactions to an array of issues where what is normatively right is deeply contestable. Support for the US Patriot Act, for instance, surely reflects in some measure a lack of commitment to civil liberties. But just as surely, the public's reactions to some extent reflect the reality of the threat and legitimacy of the lawmaking process. Civic responsibility, in democratic politics, can turn into a cat's cradle, yet the standards that citizens must satisfy in order to meet the responsibilities of democratic citizenship have to be set at a defensible level. For an example that highlights the complexity of public attitudes on issues of security and civil liberties, see Brooks and Manza 2013, 71.

the categorization principle that made it possible exacts a high price. Muslims are categorized as out of the mainstream and not transgressive, but Islamic fundamentalists are categorized as transgressive, not merely out of the mainstream. The result: limited support for their political rights. This does not conform to the idea of liberal democracy. According to this ideal, Islamic fundamentalists are entitled to these rights, without qualification. It is not merely that it is not illegal to be an Islamic fundamentalist. The issue goes far deeper. In a liberal democracy, the right to religious faith is an inalienable right. This right holds just as squarely for faiths that are in tension with the values of contemporary secular societies as for those that fit more comfortably with them. Hewing to a fundamentalist vision of Islam is no more a rejection of liberal democracy than adhering to a fundamentalist Christian or Jewish vision of their religious faith. Nor is this right qualified in any degree because representatives of a religion make provocative and even offensive speeches critical of the values of liberal democracy.

The issue, as a matter of normative democratic theory, is not whether Islamic fundamentalists should be secure in their political rights. The answer is, yes, period. The issue, as a matter of empirical democratic theory, is the basis of judgments about the rights of Islamic fundamentalists. They are warped by fear and anger. Yet the starting point for understanding why, we maintain, is what is happening in the world as it is. The avowed aim of the most publicly visible Islamic fundamentalists in Denmark, the Danish branch of Hizb ut Tahrir, is to abolish democracy in favor of a caliphate. This group's leader has been convicted of racism for anti-Semitic publications. There has been a string of convictions of Islamic fundamentalists for terrorist conspiracies— among them, bombings, assassinations, and a raid on the offices of the newspaper that published the cartoons that was designed to kill as many as possible in the style of the Mumbai attack in 2008. If the question is whether there is a reality-grounded similarity between Islamic fundamentalists and bikers, the answer is yes. This supplies all the more reason why we want to insist on the difference between reality oriented and reality warranted.

The line drawn between Islamic fundamentalists and Muslims will be sharp in some places and times, and fuzzier in other places and times.[10] We nonetheless are confident that the categories used for sorting controversial groups will, even at the furthest remove, be close cousins to the ones we have picked out. How Muslims are classified—even, one can imagine, how Islamic fundamentalists are classified—is not a law of nature. To acknowledge that the categorization of groups is not invariant, however, is not to say that it is arbitrary, and still less that it is evanescent. The results of the replication study we reported, carried out two and a half years after the original study as well as deploying independent measures, mirrored those of the primary study we undertook. In light of the continuing turmoil during this period over the threat of Islamic terror, we take this as evidence that Muslims are not readily recategorized as transgressive—not a point of minor importance considering the widespread concern over Islamophobia.[11]

Even so, the grounds for optimism about liberal democracy are also grounds for pessimism. It is the simplicity and distinctness of the differences between groups that are transgressive and those that are merely out of the mainstream that highlights points of similarity between Muslims and out-of-the-mainstream groups. But it is also the simplicity and distinctness of the dividing line that underscores the points of similarity between Islamic fundamentalists and transgressive groups. There is thus an unhappy—and as far as we can see, unavoidable—irony. Paradoxically, the same rule of judgment that protects the rights of Muslims strips Islamic fundamentalists of the protection necessary for their rights.

---

[10] We are thinking here particularly of the reporting by John Sides and Kimberly Gross (2013) of an absence of a difference in evaluations of the "dangerousness" of Muslims and Muslim Americans. This does not match the contrast between Islamic fundamentalists and Muslims, but their findings give reason to highlight the risk of the distinction we have drawn being erased by virtue of Muslims being demonized—a risk that should be dismissed. Even for our results, although it should go without saying, they show that not everyone draws a clear distinction between Muslims and Islamic fundamentalists, a nontrivial number—in our measures, on the order of one in three—dislike Muslims, and a comparable proportion perceive Muslims to be a threat. Indeed, it is not least because all three things are true that observing as much support for the civil rights of Muslims as for out-of-the-mainstream Danish groups is so striking a result.

[11] Here again, the absence of a "before" measurement stymies the inferences we can draw. Still, far better to have data from when the Cartoon Crisis dominated public attention to when it had receded from public notice than to have only the "after" measurements typical in studies of unanticipated crises.

THE COVENANT PARADOX

The second paradox of inclusion goes to the moral compact underpinning the welfare state. For many, the social equality and security of the welfare state is at the heart of the promise that a truly democratic politics owes to its citizens. Denmark has been as faithful as any country in western Europe to the values of the welfare state, notwithstanding its efforts over the last decade at increasing the efficiency of government services and containing their costs. There is overwhelming consensus in support of the core commitments of the welfare state across the whole of the ideological spectrum, as we have seen.

The moral logic of the welfare state is captured by the maxim that "duties come before rights." To US ears, the maxim may sound an odd note. The presumption is that the benefits of the welfare state are universal, which is to say unconditional. Some benefits are indeed universal, with health care being one example, and disability pensions for those unable to work on health grounds another. But not all rights to benefits are unconditional. To cite the most politically contentious instance, there is no right to social welfare state assistance. Members of the society must earn the right to this aid. They must be prepared to contribute to the welfare of the larger society before they are entitled to social welfare assistance themselves.

How is this moral maxim applied to immigrants? Unfairly, is the answer that common sense gives. Immigrants are widely perceived to be exploiting social assistance programs—in fact, to be making their decision to immigrate in order to exploit these programs, and then taking up their lives in their new country to enjoy its benefits while shirking its responsibilities. Immigrants are disproportionately likely to be on welfare. Although the stereotype of immigrants as shirkers is to some degree grounded in reality, we again want to emphasize that this is not the same thing as warranted by reality. Still, it provides a socially defensible justification for a position that immigrants are not entitled to the same measure of welfare aid as fellow Danes.

This is the truth of the matter, our results show, yet it misses the heart of the matter. The moral premise that duties come before rights imposes a temporal logic on decisions about entitlements to welfare benefits. A person must first have a fair opportunity to fulfill their duty before they can be charged with failing to perform it. Young immigrants, it follows, must have the same benefits as young Danes—for example, special assistance for the young mother so she can attend a job-training program. How could she be judged to have failed to meet her duty to contribute to the larger society if she is denied the means to do so?

It may reasonably be objected that a different logic—that of self-interest—may be at work. If immigrants don't receive training and educational opportunities, they are more likely to wind up on welfare. Danes, it follows, may be as ready to provide supportive benefits for young immigrants as for fellow Danes not out of a commitment to a social covenant but instead out of self-interest. They don't want to pay taxes to support immigrants because they didn't get the assistance necessary when they were younger to support themselves.

On its face, the self-interest hypothesis is credible. Suppose it is not merely credible but correct—that it is self-interest as opposed to a commitment to moral principle that underpins equal assistance for young immigrants and young Danes to be able to further their education. Then, though Danes may be as willing to provide the same aid to young immigrants to get ahead as to fellow Danes, it will be a different matter when it comes to the requirements for staying on welfare. They will be more likely to impose strict requirements on immigrants to continue to receive welfare. But in fact, as we saw, there is no double standard. Danes treated young immigrants and young fellow Danes alike.

The temporal sequencing, duties before rights, cuts just the other way for older immigrants, however. They have, and in still greater measure are perceived to have, stayed out of the labor force, many surely for reasons that have nothing to do with their faith or character—a lack of education or facility in speaking the language of their new country, to mention two of the most obvious. Yet the stereotype of them as shirkers opens the door to a presumption that an older immigrant has not met their obligation to the larger society and, even so, is seeking to obtain benefits from it. The phrase "opens the door" deserves highlighting. The maxim underpinning the welfare state, duties before rights, does not stimulate punitive responses to older immigrants.[12] It does legitimize them, though.

---

[12] See the discussion below of inclusive tolerance—in particular, the finding that it is those who dislike as well as disdain immigrants who take advantage of an opening to treat them differently and worse.

Hence the covenant paradox: the moral covenant undergirding the welfare state promotes equal treatment for younger immigrants, but legitimizes discrimination against older ones.

DEMOCRATIC VALUES AS A POSITIVE FORCE: INCLUSIVE TOLERANCE

Until the mid-1960s, Gunnar Myrdal's (1944) *An American Dilemma* defined the understanding of race in the United States. His book was then subjected to withering criticism, and now is largely forgotten.

Why did Myrdal's monumental work suffer this fate? The struggle for racial equality would be long and hard, he recognized. The outcome was uncertain. But he was optimistic. In the end, he believed the force of the democratic creed—liberty, equality, and fair play—would win out. In the mid-1960s, however, Myrdal's focus on values as a force for change and racial progress came to be viewed by both academics and activists as simpleminded—"sunshine sociology," as one characterization put it.[13] A nice touch: just as the civil rights movement reached its peak of success, thanks in significant measure to its appeal to the values of liberty and equality, social scientists concluded that values were of no consequence.

And in the next season of intellectual fashions, political scientists turned Myrdal upside down. The new racism, they maintained, once again had become an overpowering force in US politics precisely because it had the backing of traditional US values. To be sure, they did not have in mind the same traditional US values as Myrdal. Myrdal meant liberty, equality, and fair play. They meant individualism, among other values.[14] But the pirouette is now complete all the same. Rather than core US values being a reason for hope, they are reason for pessimism.

It was and remains right to recognize the continuing force of racial prejudice and intolerance more generally in shaping how the majority

[13] The phrase *sunshine sociology* is taken from David Southern (1955), who used it to characterize the emerging critique of Myrdal's work among academics. Much has been lost in the dismissive rejection of Myrdal's concentration on values. It does, for us, put the issue in a different context if you know that he hit on the conception of the US creed when, in Sweden, he was attempting to stiffen Swedish resistance to Nazi demands. Sunshine sociology does not do justice to Myrdal's views and still less his courage.

[14] Near the top of their list was "obedience and discipline"—possibly traditional Prussian values, yet hardly traditional US ones (e.g., Kinder and Sears 1981, 416).

treats minorities. Certainly, it has been a focus of our own research.[15] But a defining aim of this study is to recover Myrdal's insight. The values of liberal democracy have a propulsive force, he contended. We are in a position, however, to examine only a circumscribed version of his insight. We concentrate on only one moment in time, so at most we can show that democratic values are a positive force for equality, not that they are propulsive ones. No less consequentially, we hone in on only one value of a democratic politics—tolerance.

Our choice of tolerance as a focal point may seem perverse, given that tolerance has become a synonym for toleration. Tolerance goes no further than accommodation, many theorists of democracy agree; hence the patronizing references to "mere" tolerance. It is possibly instructive that "mere" tolerance is demoted to the second rank of democratic values just when intolerance once again has become among the most pressing problems in contemporary western European politics. Yet our objective is not to criticize contemporary democratic theory. Our aim is recover an older, more positive understanding of tolerance—namely, to support, nourish, and sustain.[16] This form of tolerance is affirmative, supportive, and inclusive; thus our baptizing it inclusive tolerance.

What does inclusive tolerance require? Merely thinking well of a minority is insufficient; it is necessary to treat them well, too, as we noted earlier. And what does treating minorities well call for? It means their inclusion as full members of a common community. This seems to us the right standard. Insofar as the majority treats a minority as a member of a common community, the distinction between in-group and out-group is erased. Even so, it is not appropriate to simply discard the insight that tolerance requires overcoming a reason not to be tolerant.[17] Accordingly, for a person to qualify as inclusively tolerant, they must treat minorities as members of a common community *in spite of having immediately available as well as salient a socially acceptable reason to treat them differently and worse*. There is a final consideration. The same act

---

[15] See, for example, Petersen et al. 2011b; Sniderman and Hagen 1985; Sniderman and Piazza 1993, 2002; Sniderman and Carmines 1997; Sniderman et al. 2000; Sniderman and Hagendoorn 2007; Stubager 2010.

[16] Again we acknowledge our indebtedness to Josiah Ober.

[17] This requirement is the heart of the approach of Sullivan and his colleagues. In their framework, for a person to qualify as tolerant requires them to affirm the civil rights of the group they most dislike.

can be done for different reasons, and the meaning of what was done hinges on the reason for doing it. Therefore, treating minorities well for a variety of socially acceptable or even praiseworthy motives—compassion, generosity, and charity—does not qualify as instances of inclusive tolerance. For a person to qualify as inclusively tolerant, they must treat minorities well because they think well of them. They must treat them well because they think of them as equals who deserve respect, not as powerless objects who should be pitied.

Meeting these three requirements is a minimal standard of inclusive tolerance, to be sure. More demanding ones are conceivable, such as providing immigrant minorities help above and beyond what one would supply to a native Dane because of the additional obstacles that immigrants inevitably must overcome. But a standard of "extra" help is inherently vague, and vagueness invites an excess of moral ambitiousness. Hence our choice of standards of inclusion: treating minorities as members of a common community—hardly an ungenerous standard, we would add, in a welfare state. And using equal treatment as a standard pays a bonus. Instead of having to rely on reports of subjective feelings or intentions, how people are treated is open to objective measurement. Thanks to randomized experiments, one can assess not only whether but also to what degree immigrants and native citizens, in exactly the same circumstances, are treated the same. To the extent that they are treated the same, immigrants are being included in the larger society on the same terms as native citizens.

Our aim has been to determine whether there is a positive force working in favor of minorities in addition to the negative forces working against them. Our results are consistent with this view of the ethos of contemporary liberal democracies. We are not at all suggesting that the forces working for inclusion offset, or still less prevail over, the forces working for exclusion. On the contrary, consistent with previous research, our results document strong anti-immigration sentiments. First, in the beginning of chapter 2, we saw that such sentiments were widespread in Denmark—not much more widespread than in comparable countries, but widespread nonetheless. Second, in chapter 3, we investigated the conditions under which immigrant minorities are treated differently and worse. Due to the use of randomized experiments, we demonstrated that when there is a socially defensible opportunity for treating immigrants differently and worse, a larger portion of the public favors a double standard than favors inclusion. Third—and as a last example—our goal in chapter 4 was to show that the ideological sources of anti-immigration sentiments are even stronger than has been supposed. A vast amount of evidence has established a close connection between right-wing social values and aversion to immigration. Views about economic redistribution, this research has also suggested, are not associated with such aversion. Yet an analysis of our data, backed up by analyses of every comparable data set available, reveals that a commitment to egalitarianism when *combined* with right-wing social values—as it frequently is—is in fact not only associated with aversion to immigration but also boosts hostility to even higher levels. That a commitment to a greater measure of economic equality can, in this way, strengthen the forces of exclusion is arguably yet another paradox of contemporary liberal democracy.

When we ourselves scrutinize our results, we can see no way of avoiding the conclusion that the force of ill will toward immigrants outweighs that of goodwill. It is thus all the more remarkable that in the face of demands by Muslims in other countries that the values of their faith take precedence over the values of liberal democracy, ordinary citizens nonetheless provided a solid wall of support for the civil liberties and civil rights of Muslims.

Appendix A: Timeline of the Cartoon Crisis

September 30, 2005	*Jyllands-Posten*'s publication of the twelve cartoons
October 12, 2005	Eleven ambassadors from Muslim countries request a meeting with the Danish prime minister
October 21, 2005	The prime minister rejects the ambassadors' request
October 29, 2005	The Egyptian ambassador, Mona Omar, calls on the international society to take action
November 14, 2005	A Pakistani bounty is placed on the cartoonists' heads
December 3, 2005	The first delegation of Danish imams travels to the Middle East to garner support for their opposition to the cartoons
December 7, 2005	The UN high commissioner for human rights expresses concern over the cartoons
December 17, 2005	A second imam delegation travels to the Middle East
January 7, 2006	The cartoons are reprinted in Sweden
January 20, 2006	A boycott of Danish commodities is initiated in the Middle East

January 26, 2006	Saudi Arabia initiates a recall of Muslim ambassadors from Denmark
January 29, 2006	Desecration of the Danish flag in the West Bank
February 1, 2006	The cartoons are reprinted across Europe
February 4, 2006	The organization Democratic Muslims is founded, and the Danish embassy in Damascus, Syria, is attacked
February 5, 2006	The Danish consulate in Beirut, Lebanon, is set on fire
February 9, 2006	Demonstrations of up to seven hundred thousand participants are held across the Muslim world
February 13, 2008	The cartoons are reprinted in Danish media as a response to a failed assassination attempt on Kurt Westergaard, the cartoonist who drew the picture of Mohammed with a bomb in his turban
June 2, 2008	The Danish embassy in Islamabad, Pakistan, is attacked with a car bomb, and al-Qaida claims responsibility, saying it is revenge for the cartoons
January 1, 2010	Westergaard is attacked in his home by an ax-wielding man, but survives by hiding in his bathroom

Appendix B: Description of the Main Data Set

The main data used throughout the book were collected in spring and summer 2006 by the Danish agency SFI-Survey. The data were collected in three rounds. All respondents were selected at random from the Central Office of Civil Registration, which has records of everyone living in Denmark. The sampling frame was restricted to Danish citizens aged eighteen to seventy years. The interviews were carried out by means of computer-assisted telephone interviewing (CATI). The samples were all roughly representative of the Danish population (between the ages of seventeen and seventy-one). All details of the representativeness of the data are contained in the online appendix (http://press.princeton.edu/titles/10400.html).

The details about the three rounds are as follows:

ROUND 1

Fieldwork dates: February 1–April 29, 2006. All but four interviews were conducted February 12–April 17, 2006.

Sample size: 1,919.

The minimum response rate was 67 percent (AAPOR RR1), and the respondent-level cooperation rate was 83 percent (AAPOR COOR3).

ROUND 2

Fieldwork dates: March 2–August 20, 2006. Most interviews were conducted March 2–May 31, 2006 (n = 1,798; 91.4 percent). The last group of interviews (n = 169) was conducted from June through August, as the polling company had to draw a new sample because the response rate turned out to be a bit lower than expected.

Sample size: 1,967.

The response rate was 63 percent, and the cooperation rate was 77 percent.

ROUND 3

May 6–August 27, 2006. Relatively few interviews were conducted in July and August (n = 193; 9.4 percent).

Sample size: 2,043.

The response rate was 63 percent, and the cooperation rate was 76 percent.

Appendix C: Comparison of Respondents from the Height and Aftermath of the Crisis

The data used for tracking the development in support for the rights of the eight groups come from the second round of our main study (the fieldwork was done March 2–August 20, 2006). The bulk of the interviews in this round were done March 2–May 31, 2006 (n = 1,798; 91.4 percent). The last group of interviews (n = 169) was conducted in June–August, 2006, as the polling company had to draw a new sample of individuals from the Central Person Registry because the response rate turned out to be a bit lower than expected.

To gauge the support for rights during and after the crisis, we have divided the respondents into the two time periods: March–April and May–July. This procedure, however, runs the risk of producing biased results since it is possible that the respondents interviewed in the first period are systematically different from those interviewed in the second period—if nothing else, they may have been easier to reach and persuade to take part in the interview. In the following, we investigate the extent of such differences on a range of core variables that may affect the relationships we are exploring: gender, age, level of education, county of residence, political interest, and political knowledge.

The distribution of males and females in the two subsamples appears in table A.1. As can be seen, there are no significant differences between the two subsamples.

Looking at the distribution across age in table A.2 we can observe that the March–April subsample holds fewer forty- to forty-nine-year-olds and more sixty- to seventy-year-olds than the May–July sample. Although the differences are not huge, it is relevant to correct for them in our main analyses.

TABLE A.1 The Distribution of Gender in March–April and May–July (Percent)

	March–April	May–July	Total
Male	48	51	49
Female	52	49	51
	100	100	100

Note: Total N = 1,939.

TABLE A.2 The Distribution of Age in March–April and May–July (Percent)

	March–April	May–July	Total
18–29 years	18	19	18
30–39 years	19	22	21
40–49 years	20*	25	22
50–59 years	24	21	22
60–70 years	19*	14	17
	100	100	100

Note: * indicates a significant difference at the 0.05-level. Total N = 1,939.

The breakdown on county of residence in table A.3 does, though, reveal substantially as well as statistically significant differences between the two subsamples. Thus, the table illustrates that the polling agency concentrated its efforts in different parts of the country in the two time periods. In March–April, many interviews were conducted in the eastern part of the country, particularly the Copenhagen area. Yet in May–July, interviews were concentrated in the western part of the country. These differences clearly have to be corrected in our main analyses.

On education, we also find some differences between the two periods (cf. table A.4). The March–April subsample therefore holds fewer respondents with a vocational upper secondary and more with a long-cycle tertiary education than the May–July sample. Again, the differences should be corrected in the main analyses.

Table A.5 reveals significant differences of some magnitude regarding the distribution of political interest in the two subsamples. Hence, the March–April sample holds more respondents who are very interested and fewer who are only slightly interested than the May–July sample. These differences are worth correcting, too.

TABLE A.3 The Distribution of County of Residence in March–April and May–July (Percent)

	March–April	May–July	Total
City of Copenhagen	16*	5	10
Copenhagen County	17*	5	11
Frederiksborg County	12*	4	8
Roskilde County	6*	3	4
West Zealand County	8*	2	5
Storstrøm County	6	4	5
Bornholm County	1*	0	1
Funen County	9	10	9
South Jutland County	4*	6	5
Ribe County	3	5	4
Vejle County	3*	11	7
Ringkøbing County	3*	9	6
Aarhus County	10*	14	12
Viborg County	2*	5	4
North Jutland County	1*	16	9
	100	100	100

Note: * indicates a significant difference at the 0.05-level. Total N = 1,939.

TABLE A.4 The Distribution of Education in March–April and May–July (Percent)

	March–April	May–July	Total
Only primary	17	18	17
Vocational upper secondary	38*	43	41
Short-cycle tertiary	16	15	16
Medium-cycle tertiary	16	16	16
Long-cycle tertiary	12*	8	10
	100	100	100

Note: * indicates a significant difference at the 0.05-level. Total N = 1,912.

TABLE A.5 The Distribution of Political Interest in March–April and May–July (Percent)

	March–April	May–July	Total
Very interested	23*	15	19
Somewhat interested	45	45	45
Only slightly interested	28*	34	31
Not at all interested	4	6	5
	100	100	100

Note: * indicates a significant difference at the 0.05-level. Total N = 1,928.

TABLE A.6 The Distribution of Political Knowledge in March–April and May–July (Percent)

	March–April	May–July	Total
Low knowledge	34	37	36
Medium knowledge	38	37	38
High knowledge	28	26	27
	100	100	100

Note: Total N = 1,939.

Finally, table A.6 shows no differences between the samples on political knowledge.

The overall impression of the comparisons of the two waves of our survey is that there are a number of statistically as well as substantially significant differences, which we need to take into account when analyzing the data. Thus, in order to avoid biases arising from the differences, we control all analyses involving the two time periods for the variables just examined (i.e., gender, age, county of residence, education, political interest, and political knowledge). Although there were no significant differences for gender and political knowledge, we include the variables as controls to be on the safe side.

Appendix D: Scaling and Measurement of Core Variables

Throughout the analyses we rely on a set of core variables in the form of scales, which are constructed on the basis of several individual items. Below we present the wordings of each item as well as details on the scales. In constructing the scale, we have applied the praxis of including respondents with missing values on up to two of the items on each scale. For such respondents, the missing values have been replaced with the mean value on the remaining items on the scale. "Don't know" was counted as a missing value.

ATTITUDES TOWARD IMMIGRANTS SCALE

The following items were used for the scale:

- Immigrants must be able to preach and practice their religion in Denmark freely
- Immigrants who have committed acts leading to prison sentences should be deported immediately
- Foreigners should only be able to receive Danish citizenship after they have learned to act like a Dane
- If there are not enough jobs, employers should employ Danes ahead of immigrants

The response categories were: completely agree, somewhat agree, neither-nor, somewhat disagree, completely disagree, and don't know.

The additive scale runs from 0 to 1, with 1 as the most anti-immigrant position. Cronbach's Alpha for the scale is 0.71.

CULTURAL IDEOLOGY SCALE

The following items were used for the scale:

- Violent crimes should be punished much harder than is currently the case
- Economic growth should be ensured through the expansion of industry, even if this comes at the cost of environmental interests
- As part of the War on Terror, the Danish Security and Intelligence Service should have far greater opportunities to gather information about all of us
- It would be reasonable to let a strong person take over in an economic crisis

The response categories were: completely agree, somewhat agree, neither-nor, somewhat disagree, completely disagree, and don't know.

The additive scale runs from 0 to 1, with 1 as the most right-wing position. Cronbach's Alpha for the scale is 0.53.

ECONOMIC IDEOLOGY SCALE

The following items were used for the scale:

- The state has too little control over the business world
- High incomes should be taxed more than is currently the case
- In politics, one should strive to ensure the same economic conditions for everyone, regardless of education and employment
- I am worried that the welfare state, as we know it today, is currently under threat

The response categories were: completely agree, somewhat agree, neither-nor, somewhat disagree, completely disagree, and don't know.

The additive scale runs from 0 to 1, with 1 as the most right-wing position. Cronbach's Alpha for the scale is 0.54.

GENERALIZED SOCIAL TRUST SCALE

The following items were used for the scale:

- There are not that many people you can trust completely
- Other people will exploit you if you are not careful

- Now I would like to hear whether you think you can trust most people or if you think that you can't be too careful when dealing with other people

The response categories for the first two items were: completely agree, somewhat agree, neither-nor, somewhat disagree, completely disagree, and don't know.

The response categories for the third item were: you can trust most people, it depends . . . , and you can't be too careful when dealing with other people. Cronbach's Alpha for the scale is 0.68.

References

Ackerman, Nathan, and Marie Jahoda. 1950. *Anti-Semitism and Emotional Disorders: A Psycho-Analytic Interpretation.* New York: Harper.

Alesina, Alberto, and Edward L. Glaeser. 2004. *Fighting Poverty in the US and Europe: A World of Difference.* New York: Oxford University Press.

Allport, Gordon. 1954. *The Nature of Prejudice.* Reading, MA: Addison-Wesley.

Altemeyer, Robert. 1988. *Enemies of Freedom: Understanding Right-wing Authoritarianism.* Mississauga, ON: Jossey-Bass.

Andress, Hans Jürgen, and Thorstein Heien. 2001. "Four Worlds of Welfare State Attitudes? A Comparison of Germany, Norway, and the United States." *European Sociological Review* 17:337–56.

Arkes, Hal R., and Philip E. Tetlock. 2004. "Attributions of Implicit Prejudice, or 'Would Jesse Jackson "Fail" the Implicit Association Test?'" *Psychological Inquiry* 15:257–78.

Bech Thomsen, Per. 2006. *Muhammed-krisen: Hvad skete der, hvad har vi lært?* [The Mohammed crisis: What happened, what have we learned?]. Copenhagen: People's Press.

Beskæftigelsesregion Hovedstaden og Sjælland. 2009. *Analyse af start- og kontanthjælpsmodtagere i Østdanmark* [Analysis of recipients of start help and social welfare benefits in eastern Denmark]. Report, January.

Blekesaune, Morten, and Jill Quadagno. 2003. "Public Attitudes toward Welfare State Policies: A Comparative Analysis of 24 Nations." *European Sociological Review* 19:415–27.

Blinder, Scott B. 2007. 'Dissonance Persists: Reproduction of Racial Attitudes among Post–Civil Rights Cohorts of White Americans." *American Politics Research* 35:299–335.

Blinder, Scott B., Robert Ford, and Elisabeth Ivarsflaten. 2010. "Reputational Shields and Anti-Prejudice Norms in Europe's Politics of Immigration." Paper presented at the annual meeting of the International Society of Political Psychology, San Francisco.

Borre, Ole. 1995. "Old and New Politics in Denmark." *Scandinavian Political Studies* 18:187–205.

———. 2007. "Issue Voting in Danmark, 2001–2005." In *Det nye politiske landskab: Folketingsvalget 2005 i perspektiv,* edited by Jørgen Goul Andersen, Johannes Andersen, Ole Borre, Kasper Møller Hansen, and Hans Jørgen Nielsen. Aarhus: Academica.

Borre, Ole, and Jørgen Goul Andersen. 1997. *Voting and Political Attitudes in Denmark*. Aarhus: Aarhus University Press.

Brody, Richard A. 1991. *Assessing the President: The Media, Elite Opinion, and Public Support*. Stanford, CA: Stanford University Press.

Brooks, Clem, and Jeff Manza. 2007. *Why Welfare States Persist: The Importance of Public Opinion in Democracies*. Chicago: University of Chicago Press.

———. 2013. *Whose Rights? Countererrorism and the Dark Side of America*. New York: Russell Sage Foundation Press.

Bullock, John G. 2011. "Elite Influence on Public Opinion in an Informed Electorate." *American Political Science Review* 105:496–515.

Buss, Arnold H. 1961. *The Psychology of Aggression*. New York: Wiley.

Chong, Dennis, and James N. Druckman. 2010. "Dynamic Public Opinion: Communication Effects over Time." *American Political Science Review* 104:663–80.

Cox, Robert Henry. 2001. "The Social Construction of an Imperative: Why Welfare Reform Happened in Denmark and the Netherlands But Not in Germany." *World Politics* 53:463–98.

Danish Government. 2005. *En ny start for alle—regeringens integrationsplan* [A new chance for everyone: The government's integration plan]. Copenhagen.

Davis, Darren. 2007. *Negative Liberty: Public Opinion and the Terrorist Attacks on America*. New York: Russell Sage Foundation Press.

Druckman, James N., Erik Peterson, and Rune Slothuus. 2013. "How Elite Partisan Polarization Affects Public Opinion Formation." *American Political Science Review* 107:57–79.

Duckitt, John. 2001. "A Cognitive-Motivational Theory of Ideology and Prejudice." In *Advances in Experimental Social Psychology*, edited by Mark P. Zanna. Vol. 33. San Diego: Academic Press.

Edlund, Jonas. 2009. "Attitudes towards State-Organized Welfare in Twenty-Two Countries: A Question of Convergence?" In *The International Social Survey Programme, 1984–2009: Charting the Globe*, edited by Max Haller, Roger Jowell, and Tom W. Smith. New York: Routledge.

Eger, Maureen A. 2010. "Even in Sweden: The Effect of Immigration on Support for Welfare State Spending." *European Sociological Review* 262:203–17.

Elchardus, Mark, and Bram Spruyt. 2012. "The Contemporary Contradictions of Egalitarianism." *European Political Science Review* 4:217–39.

Esping-Andersen, Gøsta. 1990. *The Three Worlds of Welfare Capitalism*. Princeton, NJ: Princeton University Press.

Feather, Norman T. 2006. "Deservingness and Emotions: Applying the Structural Model of Deservingness to the Analysis of Affective Reactions to Outcomes." *European Review of Social Psychology* 17:38–73.

Flanagan, Scott C. 1987. "Value Change in Industrial Societies." *American Political Science Review* 81:1303–19.

"Flere indvandrere i arbejde" [More immigrants in job]. 2010. *Jyllands-Posten*, April 1, sec. 1, 4.

Gelissen, John. 2000. "Popular Support for Institutionalized Solidarity: A Comparison between European Welfare States." *International Journal of Social Welfare* 9:285–300.

Gibson, James L. 1998. "A Sober Second Thought: An Experiment in Persuading Russians to Tolerate." *American Journal of Political Science* 42:819–50.

———. 2006. "Enigmas of Intolerance: Fifty Years after Stouffers's Communism, Conformity, and Civil Liberties." *Perspectives on Politics* 4:21–34.

Gibson, James L., and Amanda Gouws. 2003. *Overcoming Intolerance in South Africa: Experiments in Democratic Persuasion.* Cambridge: Cambridge University Press.

Gilens, Martin. 1999. *Why Americans Hate Welfare: Race, Media, and the Politics of Antipoverty Policy.* Chicago: University of Chicago Press.

Goren, Paul. 2013. *On Voter Competence.* New York: Oxford University Press.

Harding, John, Harold Froshansky, Bernard Kutner, and Isidor Chein. 1969. "Prejudice and Ethnic Relations." In *The Handbook of Social Psychology, Vol. 5*, edited by Gardner Lindzey and Elliot Aronson. Reading, MA: Addison-Wesley.

Harrits, Gitte Sommer. 2005. *Hvad betyder klasse? En rekonstruktion af klassebegrebet med henblik på en analyse af sammenhængen mellem klasser og politisk deltagelse i Danmark.* Aarhus: Politica.

Heit, Evan, and Stephen P. Nicholson. 2010. "The Opposite of Republican: Polarization and Political Categorization." *Cognitive Science* 34:1503–16.

Hibbing, John R., and John R. Alford. 2004. "Accepting Authoritative Decisions: Humans as Wary Cooperators." *American Journal of Political Science* 48:62–76.

Houtman, Dick, Peter Achterberg, and Anton Derks. 2008. *Farewell to the Leftist Working Class.* New Brunswick, NJ: Transaction Publishers.

Hussain, Asifa, and William Miller. 2006. *Multicultural Nationalism: Islamophobia, Anglophobia, and Devolution.* Oxford: Oxford University Press.

Inglehart, Ronald. 1977. *The Silent Revolution.* Princeton, NJ: Princeton University Press.

———. 1987. "Value Change in Industrial Society." *American Political Science Review* 81:1289–1303.

———. 1990. *Culture Shift in Advanced Industrial Society.* Princeton, NJ: Princeton University Press.

Ivarsflaten, Elisabeth, Scott Blinder, and Robert Ford. 2010. "The Anti-Racism Norm in Western European Immigration Politics: Why We Need to Consider It and How to Measure It." *Journal of Elections, Public Opinion, and Parties* 20:421–45.

Jackman, Mary R., and Michael J. Muha. 1984. "Education and Intergroup Attitudes: Moral Enlightenment, Superficial Democratic Commitment, or Ideological Refinement?" *American Sociological Review* 49:751–69.

Jæger, Mads Meier. 2009. "United But Divided: Welfare Regimes and the Level and Variance in Public Support for Redistribution." *European Sociological Review* 25:723–37.

———. 2012. "Do We All (Dis)like the Same Welfare State? Configurations of Public Support for the Welfare State in Comparative Perspective." In *Changing Social Equality: The Nordic Welfare Model in the 21st Century*, edited by Jon Kvist, Johan Fritzell, Bjørn Hvinden, and Olli Kangas. Bristol, UK: Policy Press.

Jensen, Carsten. 2010. "Issue Compensation and Right-wing Government Social Spending." *European Journal of Political Research* 49:282–99.

Jespersen, Knud J. V. 2004. *A History of Denmark.* New York: Palgrave Macmillan.

Johnston, Richard, Keith Banting, Will Kymlicka, and Stuart Soroka. 2010. "National Identity and Support for the Welfare State." *Canadian Journal of Political Science* 43:349–77.

Jost, John T., Christopher M. Federico, and Jamie L. Napier. 2009. "Political Ideology: Its Structure, Functions, and Elective Affinities." *Annual Review of Psychology* 60:307–33.

Kalkan, Kerem Ozan, Geoff Layman, and Eric Ushlaner. 2009. "A 'Band of Others'"? Attitudes toward Muslims in Contemporary American Society." *Journal of Politics* 71:847–62.

Katz, Irwin, Joyce Wakenhut, and R. Glen Hass. 1986. "Racial Ambivalence, Value Duality, and Behavior." In *Prejudice, Discrimination, and Racism*, edited by John F. Dovidio and Samuel L. Gaertner. New York: Academic Press.

Kelman, Herbert C., and Thomas F. Pettigrew. 1959. "How to Understand Prejudice." *Commentary* 28:421–36.

Kepel, Gilles. 2008. *Beyond Terror and Martyrdom*. Cambridge, MA: Belknap Press of Harvard University Press.

Kinder, Donald R. 2003. "Belief Systems after Converse." In *Electoral Democracy*, edited by Michael MacKuen and George Rabinowitz. Ann Arbor: University of Michigan Press.

Kinder, Donald R., and Cindy D. Kam. 2009. *Us against Them: Ethnocentric Foundations of American Opinion*. Chicago: University of Chicago Press.

Kinder, Donald R., and Lynn M. Sanders. 1996. *Divided by Color: Racial Politics and Democratic Ideals*. Chicago: University of Chicago Press.

Kinder, Donald R., and David O. Sears. 1981. "Prejudice and Politics: Symbolic Racism versus Racial Threats to the Good Life." *Journal of Personality and Social Psychology* 40:414–31.

Kitschelt, Herbert. 1994. *The Transformation of European Social Democracy*. Cambridge: Cambridge University Press.

———. 1995. *The Radical Right in Western Europe: A Comparative Analysis*. Ann Arbor: University of Michigan Press.

———. 2007. "Growth and Persistence of the Radical Right in Postindustrial Democracies: Advances and Challenges in Comparative Research." *West European Politics* 30:1176–206.

Klausen, Jytte. 2009. *The Cartoons That Shook the World*. New Haven, CT: Yale University Press.

Klineberg, Otto. 1968. "Prejudice: The Concept." In *Encyclopedia of the Social Sciences*, edited by David L. Sills. Vol. 12. New York: MacMillan.

Knutsen, Oddbjørn, and Staffan Kumlin. 2005. "Value Orientations and Party Choice." In *The European Voter*, edited by Jacques Thomassen. Oxford: Oxford University Press.

Krech, David, Richard Crutchfield, and Egerton Ballachey. 1962. *Individual in Society*. New York: McGraw-Hill.

Kriesi, Hanspeter, Edgar Grande, Romain Lachat, Martin Dolezal, Simon Bornschier, and Timotheos Frey. 2006. "Globalization and the Transformation of the National Political Space: Six European Countries Compared." *European Journal of Political Research* 45:921–56.

———. 2008. *Western European Politics in the Age of Globalization*. Cambridge: Cambridge University Press.

Kühle, Lene. 2006. *Moskeer i Danmark: Islam og muslimske bedesteder*. Aarhus: Forlaget Univers.

Kumlin, Staffan, and Bo Rothstein. 2005. "Making and Breaking Social Capital: The Impact of Welfare-State Institutions." *Comparative Political Studies* 38: 339–65.

Kvist, Jon, Johan Fritzell, Bjørn Hvinden, and Olli Kangas, eds. 2012. *Changing Social Equality: The Nordic Welfare Model in the 21st Century*. Bristol, UK: Policy Press.

Kymlicka, Will, and Keith Banting. 2006. "Immigration, Multiculturalism, and the Welfare State." *Ethics and International Affairs* 20:281–304.

Larsen, Christian Albrekt. 2006. *The Institutional Logic of Welfare Attitudes*. Hampshire, UK: Ashgate.

———. 2011. "Ethnic Heterogeneity and Public Support for Welfare: Is the American Experience Replicated in Britain, Sweden, and Denmark?" *Scandinavian Political Studies* 34:332–53.

"Lavere kontanthjælp skal få folk i job" [Lower welfare benefits to push people into jobs]. 2004. *Ritzaus Bureau*, January 26.

Lenz, Gabriel S. 2009. "Learning and Opinion Change, Not Priming: Reconsidering the Priming Hypothesis." *American Journal of Political Science* 53:821–37.

Lewis, Charlton T. 1890. *An Elementary Latin Dictionary*. New York: American Book Company.

"Loft over kontanthjælpen" [Ceiling on welfare benefits]. 2002. *Politiken*, October 7, sec. 1, 2.

Loftager, Jørn. 2004. *Politisk offentlighed og demokrati i Danmark*. Aarhus: Aarhus University Press.

Marcus, George E., John L. Sullivan, Elizabeth Theiss-Morse, and Sandra L. Wood. 1995. *With Malice toward Some*. New York: Cambridge University Press.

Mencken, H. L. 1926. "Notes on Journalism." *Chicago Tribune*, September 19.

Merolla, Jennifer L., and Elizabeth J. Zechmeister. 2009. *Democracy at Risk: How Terrorist Threats Affect the Public*. Chicago: University of Chicago Press.

Milner, David. 1975. *Children and Race*. Harmondsworth, UK: Penguin.

Mondak, Jeffrey J., and Mitchell S. Sanders. 2003. "Tolerance and Intolerance, 1976–1998." *American Journal of Political Science* 47:492–502.

Mudde, Cas. 2007. *Populist Radical Right Parties in Europe*. Cambridge: Cambridge University Press.

Myrdal, Gunnar. 1944. *An American Dilemma: The Negro Problem and Modern Democracy*. New York: Harper and Bros.

Mythen, Gabe, Sandra Walklate, and Fatima Khan. 2009. "I'm a Muslim, But I'm Not a Terrorist: Victimization, Risky Identities, and the Performance of Safety." *British Journal of Criminology* 49:736–54.

Nicholson, Stephen P., Evan Heit, Christopher J. Carman, and Brett Hayes. 2011. "Party Systems and the Nature of Partisan Categories." Paper presented at the American Political Science Association annual meeting, Seattle, Washington, September 1–4.

Norris, Pippa. 2005. *Radical Right: Voters and Parties in the Electoral Market.* Cambridge: Cambridge University Press.

Nunn, Clyde Z., Harry J. Crockett Jr., and J. Allen William Jr. 1978. *Tolerance for Nonconformity.* San Francisco: Jossey-Bass.

Oxley, Douglas, et al. 2008. "Political Attitudes Vary with Physiological Traits." *Science* 321:1667–70.

Page, Benjamin I., and Robert Y. Shapiro. 1992. *The Rational Public: Fifty Years of Trends in Americans' Policy Preferences.* Chicago: University of Chicago Press.

Pedersen, Peder J. 2011. *Immigration and Welfare State Cash Benefits: The Danish Case.* Odense: University Press of Southern Denmark.

Petersen, Michael Bang. 2012. "Social Welfare as Small-Scale Help: Evolutionary Psychology and the Deservingness Heuristic." *American Journal of Political Science* 56:1–16.

Petersen, Michael Bang, Rune Slothuus, Rune Stubager, and Lise Togeby. 2007a. "Eksperimenter: Et redskab i politologens værktøjskasse?" [Experiments: A tool in the political science toolbox?]. *Politica* 39:5–13.

———. 2007b. "Frihed for Loke såvel som for Thor?" [Freedom of speech for everyone?]. *Politica* 39:49–66.

———. 2007c. "Hvem fortjener velfærd? Danskernes syn på kontanthjælp til unge, ældre og indvandrere" [Who deserves welfare? Public opinion on welfare benefits to young people, senior citizens, and immigrants]. *Politica* 39:31–48.

———. 2011a. "Deservingness versus Values in Public Opinion on Welfare: The Automaticity of the Deservingness Heuristic." *European Journal of Political Research* 50:24–52.

———. 2011b. "Freedom for All? The Strength and Pliability of Political Tolerance." *British Journal of Political Science* 41:581–97.

Petersen, Michael Bang, Rune Slothuus, and Lise Togeby. 2010. "Political Parties and Value Consistency in Public Opinion Formation." *Public Opinion Quarterly* 74:530–50.

Pierson, Paul. 1994. *Dismantling the Welfare State? Reagan, Thatcher, and the Politics of Retrenchment.* Cambridge: Cambridge University Press.

———. 2001. "Post-Industrial Pressures on the Mature Welfare States." In *The New Politics of the Welfare State,* edited by Paul Pierson. Oxford: Oxford University Press.

Putnam, Robert D. 2000. *Bowling Alone: The Collapse and Revival of American Community.* New York: Simon and Schuster.

Rohrschneider, Robert. 1996. "Institutional Learning versus Value Diffusion: The Evolution of Democratic Values among Parliamentarians in Eastern and Western Germany." *Journal of Politics* 58:442–66.

Rosch, Eleanor, and Carolyn B. Mervis. 1975. "Family Resemblance: Studies in the Intrinsic Structure of Categories." *Cognitive Psychology* 7:573–605.

Rose, Arnold. 1951. *The Roots of Prejudice.* Paris: UN Educational, Scientific, and Cultural Organization.

Runnymede Trust. 1997. *Islamophobia: A Challenge for Us All.* London: Runnymede Trust.

Scanlon, Thomas M. 2003. *The Difficulty of Tolerance.* New York: Cambridge University Press.

Schultz-Nielsen, Marie Louise, Christer Gerdes, and Eskil Wadensjö. 2011. *The Significance of Immigration for Public Finances in Denmark.* Odense: University Press of Southern Denmark.

Schuman, Howard, Charlotte Steeh, Lawrence D. Bobo, and Maria Krysan. 1997. *Racial Attitudes in America: Trends and Interpretations.* Rev. ed. Cambridge, MA: Harvard University Press.

Seidenfaden, Tøger, and Rune E. Larsen. 2006. *Karikaturkrisen: En undersøgelse af baggrund og ansvar.* Copenhagen: Gyldendal.

Selznick, Gertude Jaeger, and Stephen Steinberg. 1969. *The Tenacity of Prejudice: Anti-Semitism in Contemporary America.* New York: Harper and Row.

Senik, Claudia, Holger Stichnoth, and Karine Van der Straeten. 2009. "Immigration and Natives' Attitudes towards the Welfare State: Evidence from the European Social Survey." *Social Indicators Research* 91:345–70.

Sibley, Chris G., Marc S. Wilson, and John Duckitt. 2007. "Effects of Dangerous and Competitive Worldviews on Right-wing Authoritarianism and Social Dominance Orientation over a Five-Month Period." *Political Psychology* 28: 357–71.

Sides, John, and Kimberly Gross. 2013. "Stereotypes of Muslims and Support for the War on Terror." *Journal of Politics* 75:583–98.

Simpson, George E., and J. Milton Yinger. 1985. *Racial and Cultural Minorities: An Analysis of Prejudice and Discrimination.* New York: Wiley.

Slothuus, Rune. 2010. "When Can Political Parties Lead Public Opinion? Evidence from a Natural Experiment." *Political Communication* 27:158–77.

Slothuus, Rune, and Claes H. de Vreese. 2010. "Political Parties, Motivated Reasoning, and Issue Framing Effects." *Journal of Politics* 72:630–45.

Sniderman, Paul M. 2000. "Taking Sides: A Fixed Choice Theory of Political Reasoning." In *Elements of Reason,* edited by Arthur Lupia, Mathew D. McCubbins, and Samuel L. Popkin. New York: Cambridge University Press.

———. 2011. "The Logic and Design of the Survey Experiment." In *Cambridge Handbook of Experimental Political Science,* edited by James N. Druckman, Donald P. Green, James H. Kuklinski, and Arthur Lupia. New York: Cambridge University Press.

Sniderman, Paul M., and John Bullock. 2004. "A Consistency Theory of Public Opinion and Political Choice: The Hypothesis of Menu Dependence." In *Studies in Public Opinion,* edited by William E. Saris and Paul M. Sniderman. Princeton, NJ: Princeton University Press.

Sniderman, Paul M., and Edward G. Carmines. 1997. *Reaching beyond Race.* Cambridge, MA: Harvard University Press.

Sniderman, Paul M., Joseph F. Fletcher, Peter H. Russell, and Philip E. Tetlock. 1996. *The Clash of Rights: Liberty, Equality, and Legitimacy in Pluralist Democracy.* New Haven, CT: Yale University Press.

Sniderman, Paul M., and Michael G. Hagen. 1985. *Race and Inequality: A Study in American Values.* Chatham, NJ: Chatham House.

Sniderman, Paul M., Michael G. Hagen, Philip E. Tetlock, and Henry E. Brady. "Reasoning Chains: Causal Models of Policy Reasoning in Mass Publics." *British Journal of Political Science* 16 (1986): 405–430.

Sniderman, Paul M., and Louk Hagendoorn. 2007. *When Ways of Life Collide: Multiculturalism and Its Discontents in the Netherlands.* Princeton, NJ: Princeton University Press.

Sniderman, Paul M., and Thomas Piazza. 1993. *The Scar of Race.* Cambridge, MA: Belknap Press of Harvard University Press.

———. 2002. *Black Pride and Black Prejudice.* Princeton, NJ: Princeton University Press.

Sniderman, Paul M., Pierangelo Peri, Rui J. P. de Figueiredo Jr., and Thomas Piazza. 2000. *The Outsider: Prejudice and Politics in Italy.* Princeton, NJ: Princeton University Press.

Sniderman, Paul M., and Edward H. Stiglitz. 2008. "Race and the Moral Character of the Modern American Experience." *The Forum: A Journal of Applied Research in Contemporary Politics* 6.

Sniderman, Paul M., Philip E. Tetlock, James M. Glaser, Donald P. Green, and Michael Hout. 1989. "Principled Tolerance and the American Mass Public." *British Journal of Political Science* 19:25–45.

Son Hing, Leanne S., Greg A. Chung-Yan, Leah K. Hamilton, and Mark P. Zanna. 2008. "A Two-dimensional Model That Employs Explicit and Implicit Attitudes to Characterize Prejudice." *Journal of Personality and Social Psychology* 94:971–87.

Sønderskov, Kim Mannemar. 2011. "Does Generalized Social Trust Lead to Associational Membership? Unraveling a Bowl of Well-Tossed Spaghetti." *European Sociological Review* 27: 419–34.

Southern, David W. 1995. "An American Dilemma after Fifty Years: Putting the Myrdal Study and Black-White Relations in Perspective." *History Teacher* 28: 227–53.

Stouffer, Samuel A. 1955. *Communism, Conformity, and Civil Liberties: A Cross-section of the Nation Speaks Its Mind.* Garden City, NY: Doubleday and Co.

Stubager, Rune. 2006. *The Education Cleavage.* Aarhus: Politica.

———. 2010. "The Development of the Education Cleavage: Denmark as a Critical Case." *West European Politics* 33:505–33.

Stubager, Rune, Jakob Holm, Maja Smidstrup, and Katrine Kramb. 2013. *Danske vælgere 1971–2011. En oversigt over udviklingen i vælgernes holdninger mv.* Aarhus: Institut for Statskundskab.

Sullivan, John L., James E. Piereson, and George E. Marcus. 1982. *Political Tolerance and American Democracy.* Chicago: University of Chicago Press.

"De svage hårdt presset af reform" [The vulnerable under pressure by reform]. 2003. *Politiken,* June 16, sec. 1, 1.

Svallfors, Stefan. 1997. "Worlds of Welfare and Attitudes to Redistribution: A Comparison of Eight Western Nations." *European Sociological Review* 13:283–304.

———. 2012. *Contested Welfare States: Welfare Attitudes in Europe and Beyond.* Stanford, CA: Stanford University Press.

Tesler, Michael, and David O. Sears. 2010. *Obama's Race: The 2008 Election and the Dream of a Post-Racial America.* Chicago: University of Chicago Press.

Togeby, Lise. 2004. *Man har et standpunkt.* Aarhus: Aarhus University Press.

Treier, Shawn, and D. Sunshine Hillygus. 2009. "The Nature of Political Ideology in the Contemporary Electorate." *Public Opinion Quarterly* 73:679–703.

Uslaner, Eric M. 2002. *The Moral Foundations of Trust.* New York: Cambridge University Press.

van der Brug, Wouter, and Meindert Fennema. 2007. "The Support Base of Anti-immigration Parties in the Enlarged European Union States." In *European Elections after Eastern Enlargement: Preliminary Results of the European Elections Study 2004,* edited by Michael Marsh, Slava Mikhaylov, and Hermann Schmitt. Connex Report Series No. 1. Mannheim: Mannheim Centre for European Social Research.

van der Brug, Wouter, and Joost van Spanje. 2009. "Immigration, Europe, and the 'New' Cultural Dimension." *European Journal of Political Research* 48:309–34.

van Kersbergen, Kees, and Barbara Vis. 2014. *Comparative Welfare State Politics: Development, Opportunities, and Reform.* Cambridge: Cambridge University Press.

van Oorschot, Wim. 2000. "Who Should Get What, and Why? On Deservingness Criteria and the Conditionality of Solidarity among the Public." *Policy and Politics* 28:33–48.

Weiner, Bernard. 1995. *Judgments of Responsibility.* New York: Guilford Press.

Williams, Bernard. 2005. *In the Beginning Was the Deed.* Princeton, NJ: Princeton University Press.

Wolfe, Alan, and Jytte Klausen. 1997. "Identity Politics and the Welfare State." *Social Philosophy and Policy* 2:231–55.

Zak, Paul J. 2007. "The Neuroeconomics of Trust." In *Renaissance in Behavioral Economics,* edited by Roger Frantz. Florence, KY: Routledge.

Zaller, John. 1992. *The Nature and Origins of Mass Opinion.* Cambridge: Cambridge University Press.

Index

abortion, 24–25
Achterberg, Peter, 91n12, 104n23
Ackerman, Nathan, 119
Alesina, Alberto, 53
Alford, John R., 123n7
Allport, Gordon, 119
Altemeyer, Robert, 93nn16 and 17
American Dilemma, An (Myrdal), 151
Andersen, Jørgen Goul, 89n7, 92n14
Andress, Hans Jürgen, 55n8
anti-immigration politics: authoritarianism and, 89–103, 108–16 Christians
   and, 105n24; citizenship and, 94n19;
   claim of, 83; class distinctions and,
   85; combustibility model and, 83, 87,
   94–99, 108–9, 113–16; communitarianism and, 104–14; Danish People's Party
   and, 84, 88n4, 90f, 91, 95t, 96–97,
   98t, 100f, 102f, 103f, 110f, 111f, 113f,
   114; electorate and, 90, 96–97, 99,
   105; elitism and, 85; established model
   and, 93–95; flash point conjecture and,
   96–99; historical perspective on, 83–99;
   ideological bases of, 82, 84, 87–116;
   income and, 88n4, 92; John S. case
   study and, 84–87, 110–12; marginalization and, 106–14; political fault-lines
   and, 88n6, 114–16; political Left and,
   83, 87–91, 95, 99–109, 113–14, 115f;
   political Right and, 83, 87–91, 95,
   99–104, 109, 114; radicals and, 82,
   114; redistribution and, 84, 88–101,
   102f, 103f, 109, 110f, 111f, 113–16,
   154; Social Democrats and, 84, 90t, 91,
   112n34, 115f, 116; Social Liberals and,
   90f, 91, 112n34, 115f; standard model
   and, 87, 89, 92; starting point for

analysis of, 99–104; taxes and, 88, 92,
   112n34; tolerance and, 83, 88n6, 106;
   trust and, 109, 110f; values and, 82–99,
   104–9, 114; welfare state and, 83, 88,
   91n13, 104, 107–8
anti-Semitism, 18, 121, 121n4, 147
apologies, 3, 8, 10–11, 36–37, 143
Arkes, Hal R., 131n14
assassination: Cartoon Crisis and, 2, 10,
   156; civil rights and, 10, 16–17, 37;
   democratic impulse and, 142, 147;
   imam-sponsored, 37
attitudes toward immigrants scale, 163
Austria, 82
authoritarianism: anti-immigration
   politics and, 89–103, 108–16; inclusive
   tolerance and, 136
Autonome, 25–28, 29t, 45t, 48, 49t, 50t,
   145

Ballachey, Egerton, 119
Banting, Keith, 54
Becket, Thomas, 51
Belgium, 82
bikers, 22, 25–29, 45t, 48, 49t, 50t,
   145–47
bipolarity hypothesis, 121–22
blasphemy: Cartoon Crisis and, 15, 18n9;
   civil rights and, 15, 18n9, 36; Serrano
   exhibition and, 4
Blekesaune, Morten, 55n8
Blinder, Scott, 121n5
bombs, 1–2, 11, 16, 25, 31, 147, 156
born-again Christians: categorization hypothesis and, 144–46; civil rights and,
   8, 24–28, 29t, 34, 45t, 48–51; democratic impulse and, 143–46; inclusive

born-again Christians (*continued*)
tolerance and, 125t, 126, 128; school
funding and, 25n22
Borre, Ole, 89n7, 92n14, 93n18, 105n28
boycotts, 4–5, 10, 37, 142, 155
Brady, Henry E., 64n19
Brody, Richard, 38n34
Brooks, Clem, 4n3, 23n19, 55n9, 142n2,
146n9
Bullock, John G., 44n41, 45n42, 57n13
Buss, Arnold H., 119

Caesar, Julius, 118
caliphates, 18, 147
Camre, Mogens, 36
Carmines, Edward G., 152n15
Cartoon Crisis: assassination attempts
and, 2, 156; blasphemy and, 15, 18n9;
boycott of Danish goods and, 4–5, 10,
37, 142, 155; censorship and, 1–3,
35; civil rights and, 9–10, 15, 18, 23,
30–38, 40f, 41, 46–48; demanded/
refused apology for, 3, 8, 10–11,
36–37, 143; democratic impulse and,
142–43, 147, 148n11; economic vs.
social values and, 97; embassy burn-
ings and, 4, 8, 10, 34, 35f, 37, 142,
146, 156; fatwas and, 10, 146; fear of
violence from, 2; imams and, 10–11,
16, 18n9, 19, 36–37, 142, 146, 155;
"just below the surface" hypothesis
and, 30–34; *Jyllands-Posten* and, 1, 35f,
38n35, 40f, 155; logic of reciprocity
and, 46–50; Mohammed satire and,
1–5, 8–10, 15, 18, 23, 30–38, 40f,
41f, 46–48, 97, 142–43, 147, 148n11,
155–56; narrative line of, 3–4; orange
metaphor and, 1; partisan elite framing
and, 38–40; pattern of media coverage
and, 34–40; and reprinting of cartoons,
37, 155–56; respondent comparison
data on, 159–62; study criteria for, 2–5;
terrorism and, 1–2, 156; timeline of,
155–56; top-down politics and, 41–46;
Westergaard and, 156
categorization hypothesis: born-again
Christians and, 144–46; civil rights
and, 15–21, 24, 26, 28; democratic
impulse and, 144–48; ethnocentrism
and, 16–17; Islamophobia and, 15–20;
tolerance and, 144–45

censorship, 1–3, 35
Center-Left, 56, 76n37
Center-Right: anti-immigration politics
and, 90f, 115f; inclusive tolerance and,
138; welfare state and, 58t, 59, 60t, 61,
65t, 66, 69t, 72t, 73, 74t, 78t, 80t
chauvinism, 3
Chong, Dennis, 46n43
Christians: anti-immigration politics and,
105n24; born-again, 8, 24–28, 29t, 34,
45t, 48–51, 125t, 126, 128, 143–46;
civil rights and, 8, 24–28, 29t, 34,
45t, 48–51; democratic impulse and,
143–47; distinctness of category boundaries and, 24–28; inclusive tolerance
and, 125t, 126, 128; Serrano exhibition
and, 4
citizenship, 163; anti-immigration politics
and, 94n19; civil rights and, 32f,
33–34, 47; democratic, xiii, 5, 12, 17,
47, 143–44, 146n9; inclusive tolerance
and, 122, 124
civil liberties, 2, 6, 8; clash of rights and,
28; democratic impulse and, 141n1,
143–45, 146n9, 154; timing and, 4–5;
tolerance and, 117n1, 128–29
civil rights: assassination and, 10, 16–17,
37; Autonome and, 25–28, 29t, 45t, 48,
49t, 50t; bikers and, 22, 25–29, 45t,
48, 49t, 50t; blasphemy and, 15, 18n9,
36; Cartoon Crisis and, 9–10, 15, 18,
23, 30–38, 40f, 41, 46–48; categorization hypothesis and, 15–21, 24, 26, 28,
144–48; Christians and, 8, 24–28, 29t,
34, 45t, 48–51; citizenship and, 32f,
33–34, 47; Danish People's Party and,
36, 40–42; discrimination and, 28–30
(*see also* discrimination); distinctness
of category boundaries and, 24–28;
economic issues and, 16; elitism and,
38–40, 42, 44–46; ethnocentrism and,
16–17; freedom of expression and,
3, 15, 31, 47, 126, 144; freedom of
religion and, 24, 34; freedom of speech
and, 3, 5, 10–11, 35–47, 146n9; ideology and, 25; immigrants and, 11–20,
23, 31–34, 37, 42, 50–51; Islamic
fundamentalists and, 20–30, 34, 45t,
47, 49t, 50; "just below the surface" hypothesis and, 30–34; logic of reciprocity and, 46–50; multiculturalism and,